Wight Air Wrecks

WAR

When the bloom is off the garden

And I'm fighting in the sky

When the lawns and flowerbeds harden

And when the weak birds starve and die

The death roll will grow longer

Eyes will be moist and red

And the more I kill , The longer

Shall I miss friends who are dead.

Pilot Officer A.N.C. Wier. DFC
145 Squadron, Based at Tangmere.
Killed in Action, Ventnor; 7 November 1940.

From 'Verses of a Fighter Pilot' Published by Faber; London 1941.

Wight Air Wrecks

A. T. GILLIAM

TEMPUS

First published 2002

PUBLISHED IN THE UNITED KINGDOM BY:
Tempus Publishing Ltd
The Mill, Brimscombe Port
Stroud, Gloucestershire GL5 2QG
www.tempus-publishing.com

PUBLISHED IN THE UNITED STATES OF AMERICA BY:
Tempus Publishing Inc.
2 Cumberland Street
Charleston, SC 29401
www.tempuspublishing.com

British Library Cataloguing in Publication Data.
A catalogue record for this book is available from the British Library.

ISBN 0 7524 2376 2

Typesetting and origination by Tempus Publishing.
PRINTED AND BOUND IN GREAT BRITAIN.

Contents

Preface

The Isle of Wight is a small island covering approximately 145 square miles lying six miles off the coast of Southern England. Despite its relatively small size it has witnessed the premature demise of a large number of military aircraft, particularly during the Second World War.

This is perhaps not surprising given its proximity to important strategic mainland targets, such as Southampton docks, Portsmouth Naval dockyard and the many factories in and around these cities. In fact the Island itself had many important targets, several of which had been secretly photographed from German reconnaissance flights prior to the start of the war. These included the early warning radar stations at Ventnor, Bembridge, St Lawrence and Apse Heath, J.S. White's shipyard at Cowes and several 'shadow' factories producing aircraft parts and even whole aircraft. Large garrisons of troops, anti-aircraft batteries, and the many other military establishments on the Island also drew the attention of the aerial armadas.

Whilst the Island itself had no military airfields, several important airfields along the adjacent Hampshire, Sussex and Dorset coastal areas launched a spirited defence against the bomber streams during the Battle of Britain and later against aerial attacks on both land targets and the large amount of coastal shipping and convoys that passed in the English Channel, the resulting dogfights claiming many victims. The Island may also have been the first welcome sight of land for damaged aircraft struggling back from raids over occupied territory or from the furious dogfights that took place over the Channel.

Although the air battles of the Second World War brought about the majority of the incidents, many others have occurred in peacetime due to mechanical failures or possible design faults occurring during testing of prototypes built on the Island or due to pilot error or perhaps just bad luck or inexperience on the part of the aircrews that trained extensively in this area.

The Island's geographical features have also played their part in claiming aerial victims, several aircraft having fallen prey to its fog shrouded hills and its sudden and unyielding cliffs rising sharply from the sea.

This book seeks to chronicle the military aircraft that, from the early pioneering flights of Messrs J.S. White and Samuel Saunders of Cowes through the wartime conflicts and up to the present day, have crashed either onto the Island or into the coastal waters surrounding it; and to provide a tribute to the triumph and the tragedy that goes hand in hand with prototype development, test flying and the savagery of modern air warfare.

Hopefully it achieves a balance between a 'dry' statistical monologue and a more personalised insight into modern local history, which may promote further debate and research. I have endeavoured to include as many photographs as possible into the work; however, few photos of local crashes seem to have been taken, especially during the war years. This may have been because private photography was prohibited during this period and the Island was possibly a little remote for 'official' Ministry photographers to travel to. Therefore the majority of the included photographs show typical examples of the aircraft described.

The research and investigative work that has gone into its creation has been as thorough as the author's time and ability allows. However any publication which deals with such a large number of incidents spread over a span of some eighty years has of necessity to contain some anomalies and sketchy reports. As time goes by more and more trails go cold and more and more leads turn into blind alleys. Many sources, both official and unofficial are contradictory, confusing or just plain incorrect.

Some details have come to light via the activities of Aircraft Archaeology Groups and throughout this book various references will be found to 'digs' carried out at crash sites. These groups research crash sites exhaustively. If they consider that sufficient wreckage may have been left at the crash site by the wartime recovery crews, they may undertake the difficult task of excavating remains of aircraft which, depending on crash speed and soil conditions, could have penetrated the ground to a depth of twenty to thirty feet. Painstaking study of recovered components can reveal manufacturer's nameplates or serial numbers, squadron markings or personal effects, which can lead to a positive identification of an aircraft, and/or its crew. It should perhaps be pointed out that the excavation of any crashed aircraft is not an activity that should be undertaken lightly; many wrecks may still contain unexploded ordnance, pressurised oxygen cylinders, large quantities of fuel or even on rare occasions human remains.

From a legal viewpoint, all military crash sites are now protected by legislation and can only be excavated within strict guidelines and upon the issue of a licence by the Ministry of Defence. Secondly, virtually all crash sites are on private property and it is therefore important to obtain the landowner's permission before venturing onto any land even if only to view the area of a crash site.

The author would be pleased to receive comments or further information on any of the incidents that this work contains or indeed on any that have been missed out.

Acknowledgements

The research and production of this book has been a very long process which could quite easily have fallen by the wayside several times without the interest, enthusiasm and tolerance of a great many people; in fact such was the response that there are far too many to mention individually. Therefore, I sincerely hope that no one who has contributed in any way to this work will feel snubbed if they are not personally mentioned. Your assistance has been a valued contribution. It is an undeniable morale booster to get an interested reply from the large number of enquiries I have badgered people with, even if the answer is, 'Sorry I can't help but good luck anyway.' Many thanks also to the army of people who, knowing of the project, just simply asked, 'How is it going?'

Amongst those individuals and organisations who command a personal mention are: The counter staff at the *Isle of Wight County Press* for assisting my many hours of pouring over their micro-fiche records. Mr Peter Dimmick and the staff at the Southampton Hall of Aviation, Mr Barry Price for allowing me access to the records and notes of his late father in law, H.J.T. Leal. Air Vice Marshal A.D. Dick CB CBE AFC MA FRAeS RAF (Retd), for providing a detailed account of the loss of the Mk I Javelin from which he was forced to eject whilst over the Island. Air Britain Historians, GKN Westland and Blackburn aircraft for the supply of photographs. Mr L. Hayward of Middlesex; Mr J. Harris of Bedford; Mr R. Corby of Northants; Mr J. Farrington of Carisbrooke; Mr D. Kent of Sandown; Mr A. Saunders of Hastings; Mr P. Newberry of Portsmouth; Mr T. Jennings of Ryde and Mr S. Vizard of Kent for the amount and quality of information they supplied.

Special thanks also goes to Bob Pakes for encouragement, proof reading and for the use of his photocopier (although he probably didn't realise how many times!) and of course to my wife and family for tolerating my hundreds of hours sat in front of the computer screen, the trips out to crash sites, my impatience when something expected in the post that day fails to materialise and for sitting patiently through the long late night phone calls from fellow aviation enthusiasts (why do aircraft enthusiasts only use the phone late at night?)

I sincerely hope that those who read this work gain as much pleasure from it as I did from producing it.

Chapter One

The Pioneers

May 1913 to August 1939

The Island's aerial history started in earnest during the second decade of this century. The well-known and respected shipyard of J.S. White & Co. decided to extend their expertise in naval shipbuilding into the new-fangled art of naval aviation.

Their first attempt at aviation design resulted in the construction of the 'Seaplane No.1', the maiden flight of which ended almost as soon as it started on 13 May 1913. The pilot, Howard Wright, who, although an experienced aviator, was making his first attempt at a flight from water, stalled on take off and plunged inverted back onto the water from an altitude of around forty feet, throwing himself out of the aircraft and suffering back injuries and bruising. The wreckage was towed back to the East Cowes works from where it had been launched for inspection, but the damage was considered so severe as to 'necessitate the complete reconstruction' of the aircraft. Several theories were put forward to explain the crash ranging from strong winds, through failure of the elevator to an overly powerful engine. No official explanation was ever given.

This was in fact the second incident inside a month at Cowes. On 15 April a broadly similar crash had taken place. This incident involved a machine constructed by Bristol's and launched from the yard of another respected boat-building firm who where experimenting with aircraft, that of S.E. Saunders of Cowes. The pilot, a Mr H.T. Bustead, set off at around 05.00hrs taxiing down the river Medina for the open waters beyond Cowes harbour where a take off was achieved and his flight set off in the direction of Southampton. Contemporary reports state that he set off at a rapid rate but at no great height. When about halfway between Cowes and Calshot his engine began spluttering and the loss of power caused a rapid descent onto the 'broken' water, the impact smashing the bottom of the single float and causing it to break away. Mr Bustead was thrown out of the machine into the sea from where he and the wreckage of his machine were rescued some thirty minutes later by Capt. Williams and his crew aboard Steam Hopper No.64 operating in Southampton Water and subsequently transferred back to Cowes. Apart from the effects of cold from his time in the water he apparently sustained no injuries and even gave an interview to the *Isle of Wight County Press* at 09.00hrs that morning over breakfast at the Fountain hotel where he had based himself.

White's tried again in July of that year. The badly damaged 'Seaplane No.1' had been extensively rebuilt and modified to become 'Seaplane No.2'. This time its designer and unsuccessful pilot from the first attempt decided to watch from the company launch and the services of another experienced aviator, a Mr F.P. Raynham were sought. Shortly after half past six on the morning of 10 July the aircraft began its westerly take off run towards the Royal Yacht Squadron and Gurnard. At about Egypt Point the aircraft was seen to lift from the sea and started to execute a turn. Unfortunately it had insufficient altitude and one of its wing tips caught the water and turned the aircraft onto its side and dropped it into the sea. Raynham jumped clear and was unhurt; the wreckage was salvaged by a Trinity House vessel and once again returned in a badly damaged state to J.S. White's yard.

Strictly speaking these first aircraft were not military aircraft; for such was the infancy of flying at this time, that really there was no such thing as a true military aircraft. However, private ventures such as these were beyond the means of all but the very wealthy and if they were to be an economic success would need to taken up by an organisation with considerable purchasing power such as the War Department.

September 1916 saw J.S. White's underway with test flights of their private venture fighter. The White's Quadraplane had been completed in early August of that year and test flights were being carried out from the new airfield that the company had constructed on sixty acres of land at Somerton, during one of these flights White's chief test pilot Ralph Lashmar experienced mechanical problems with the machine and attempted to return to the airfield. Unfortunately the aircraft was unable to make the distance and, during a hurried emergency landing short of the airfield, the machine overturned and was wrecked, the pilot escaping without serious injury.

He was not to be so lucky again. Just days after the Quadraplane incident, on 7 September 1916 Ralph was at the controls of the much larger White's Landplane Bomber prototype, serial no 9841. With him on this occasion, which was to be only the prototype's second flight, was his brother Allan who was to act as observer. The flight commenced around 12.45hrs and according to contemporary reports went well at first, mirroring the maiden flight which had taken place the day before. Shortly before 13.00hrs as the aircraft was descending; disaster struck. The large bomber went out of control and crashed to the ground in a field on the edge of Ruffins Copse at Cockleton Lane, Gurnard. Ralph was killed instantly, his brother Allan was critically injured and died before medical help could be summoned. The subsequent inquest failed to find a conclusive cause of the accident, various theories were put forward including mechanical failure of the wings, but two government inspectors who examined the wreckage following the accident discounted this. The inquest heard that the machine had risen to an altitude of some 6,000ft where it had shut down its engine and had commenced a series of gliding turns. When it was at about 600ft the pilot opened up the engine and was starting another circuit when something went wrong and the aircraft entered into a spiral dive followed by a side-slip into the ground. William Wyatt, a dairyman who had witnessed the flight and subsequent crash at close quarters said that he had heard a 'pop' and saw the wings sag downwards followed by a whistling noise as the plane passed him. He felt that the pilot was still in control and would have pulled out given more altitude, although this was not a view upheld by the experts at the inquest.

The Lashmar brothers, part of a large and well-respected local family, were buried at Whippingham churchyard; their broken propeller forming their tombstone.

Six months later, on 31 March 1917, White's suffered their fourth crash. Marcus D. Manton had been taken on as chief test pilot to replace Ralph Lashmar and was test flying the rebuilt Quadraplane. This aircraft was a completely new version of the original, only the engine and a few small components had been salvaged and reused from the first aircraft. Its wing span had been increased and its chord decreased slightly to give better performance and downward vision and the undercarriage lengthened and strengthened to improve ground handling. By all accounts the aircraft performed fairly well; earlier test flights undertaken by a RNAS pilot by the name of Evans had seen the aircraft looping, rolling and zooming all over the sky to such an extent that the designer Howard Wright was heard to comment that 'he should not be doing that with that machine.' During one flight, Manton felt the whole wing cell structure shift and, unable to regain the airfield, he crash-landed on the edge of the reservoir adjacent to the cemetery at Somerton. Manton escaped serious injury but the aircraft was again badly damaged.

The *Isle of Wight County Press* of 1 April 1919, reported briefly on the crash of an Avro niplane★ carrying two RAF officers. The aircraft, which was reported to have taken off from Somerton, suffered engine failure whilst at an altitude of around 200ft. The pilot had little chance to select a suitable landing site and having narrowly missed two houses he force-landed in a small meadow at Buckberry on the outskirts of Newport. The crash tore away the undercarriage and buried the nose of the machine into the soft soil, the two officers being apparently unhurt. The wreckage was dismantled and taken away but not before it had become a brief 'tourist attraction'.

Almost a year to the day later another Avro machine was lost. This was Avro 504K, serial E3800, from the Special Experimental Flight based at Fort Grange, Gosport. It was reported as having spun out of low cloud and plunged into the sea off Gilkicker Point, Gosport on 23 April 1920.

Flat calm weather was ironically the cause of the next loss. Whilst good weather is generally an advantage to flying, it is not always so good for sea-borne take-offs. Early flying boats were generally under-powered and often needed a little choppy water in order to break the suction between hull and water on take off. On 12 December 1923, Felixstowe F2A, serial N4570, from 480 Flt, crashed whilst attempting a take-off from 'glassy' water off Cowes. The *Isle of Wight County Press* for that weekend reported that passengers on the 09.40hrs Southampton ferry *Princess Beatrice* watched as the Captain lowered a boat to rescue the seaplane's crew of P/O Collins, Lts Askew and Walton and two other unidentified crewmen who were clinging to the wreckage. The ferry's lifeboat put the airmen, who had all survived the ordeal with no more than a soaking, ashore at Calshot air station whilst the wreckage of the seaplane was towed to Calshot by an RAF launch.

A second F2A was Written off Charge (w.o.c) when it made a tail-heavy forced landing in the Solent on 15 May 1924. This machine was N4499 based at the then RAF base at Calshot.

Avro 504K Training Aircraft. (Air Britain)

Two months later on 14 July another Felixstowe aircraft came to grief in the area. This was the larger F5 seaplane N4120 that was reported as force landing at Cowes.

The first fatal Island accident involving a serving RAF pilot occurred on 17 August 1926 at Hulverstone Down, near Brook and tragically took the life of twenty-six-year-old Lt John Leslie Llewellyn-Rees, a Royal Marine officer serving with the RAF and based at Gosport air base. His aircraft was one of a formation of three Blackburn Darts on a training flight over the Island and was lost after entering a bank of fog. His flight leader, Lt Campbell, and the other member of the flight, Lt Wootten, entered the fog bank in loose formation with Rees, but on emerging from the other side realised Rees's machine was missing.

They turned round and flew back through the fog bank but saw no sign of him and assumed he must have returned to base. The flight had commenced at 14.40hrs that afternoon and was to have been of approximately forty minutes duration; the aircraft entered the fog bank around 15.00hrs and returned to Gosport at 15.40hrs, where upon finding that Rees had not returned to base they reported the incident. The flight commanding officer Flg-Off A.H.J. Howlett waited for a further five minutes and then took off to search for the missing pilot. This first search ran into thick fog over Newtown and had to be abandoned.

At 17.20hrs the weather had improved and Howlett took off for a second search. He flew out over the Needles and over the Island along the line of the Downs and eventually saw the wreckage of N9799 on a hilltop. A low pass over the site showed no sign of movement. Flg-Off Howlett landed his aircraft in a field near Shalcombe and in the company of Messrs Hooker and Udel from Chessel farm, made his way to the crash site.

On arrival they found the unfortunate pilot still strapped into the aircraft which had broken in two. The position of the wreckage and marks on the ground indicated that the machine had impacted the ridge of the hill in a gliding attitude, rather than vertically, and had bounced about 20ft after the first impact. Although it had taken nearly three hours for anybody to find the crash the inquest found that the evidence indicated the pilot had been killed instantly by massive concussion caused by the impact; other than his nose, no bones were broken.

The Coroner concluded that the evidence suggested that on entering the fog bank Rees's altimeter would have been reading around 900ft and in descending to try and escape the fog he struck the ridge of the hill, which at that point was about 700ft. He had evidently not realised that the hills in that area were so high. Had he been around 20ft higher he would almost certainly have cleared the high ground.

11 March 1929 saw the loss of another Blackburn Dart. Details of this incident are very limited. The aircraft, S1129, force-landed in the Solent while practising carrier deck landings. Its pilot, Sqdn Ldr B.H.M. Kendall was uninjured.

'Air Fatality off the Island' was the *Isle of Wight County Press* headline for a short report on the loss of a Hawker Osprey, serial K3631, based at Gosport, which whilst on exercise off the north east coast of the Island plunged into the sea, seven miles south of the Nab Tower on 5 March 1935. The incident was witnessed from the battle cruiser HMS *Hood* that was on sea trials in the Solent following repairs. A boat was launched immediately from the *Hood* but by the time it had arrived at the scene, the wreckage had sunk. The body of the pilot, Sub-Lt Nigel Radcliffe Williams, was recovered from the sea and taken to the Royal Naval Hospital at Haslar (Gosport). No trace was found of the second crewmember, Leading Aircraftsman Henry John Atkinson, who was presumed to have sunk with the aircraft. The accident was apparently caused by the dinghy storage cover breaking loose in flight and lodging on the tail thus fouling the controls.

At 11.15 a.m on 22 June 1936 the French liner *Normandie* received an unexpected visitor. A Blackburn Baffin, S1562, of 'A' flight from RAF Gosport was one of a flight of five on a training sortie in the Solent when its pilot spotted the liner and decided on a closer inspection. *Normandie* was en-route for Le Havre from New York and had ove-to in Ryde Roads, about a mile off the end of Ryde pier, to unload a deck cargo of cars onto a tender via her forward derrick. A local boat proprietor, whose vessel was about 250yds from the *Normandie* at the time of the crash, reported that 'The planes came swooping down with a terrific noise and one appeared to hit the forestay and turned a complete somersault landing on the bows as if she had been placed there.'

Large crowds of holidaymakers and locals witnessed the incident. Lt G.K. Horsey RN who was flying alone in the Baffin was reported by these onlookers to have circled the ship three times at low altitude before he got into difficulties. As he flew

Blackburn Dart, serial S1129. Shown c.1929 during maintenance. (Blackburn Archives)

along the starboard side of the ship on his third circuit he seemed to get very close to *Normandie's* funnels and suddenly lost control. The aircraft narrowly missed several obstructions on the forward structure of the ship before pitching over the rail of the promenade deck and striking the derrick. The blow to the derrick swung it back inboard and wrenched the car that was being off-loaded from its cable, fortunately for the men in the tender positioned below it fell back onto the deck and not onto them.

The impact tore off both upper and lower starboard wings and spun the Baffin through 360 degrees to leave it upright but with its tail pointing towards the bows of the ship which were scant feet away. The undercarriage was also torn away in the crash but the rest of the fuselage remained intact and the pilot stepped unhurt from the wreckage to be taken to the bridge to offer his apologies to *Normandie's* Captain.

The *Normandie* had to sail with the tide and so there was no time to recover the wrecked aircraft or for that matter the car which had been knocked from the derrick by the crash and now hung precariously over the ship's rail. The Captain put Lt Horsey ashore and departed for Le Havre with the wrecked Baffin, the damaged car of Capt. Arthur Evans MP and the rest of the cars that had been due for off loading, all of which had to be taken onto the French port. Questions were asked in the House of Commons on the following Tuesday about this incident after Sir P. Sassoon** stated that an RAF team had been despatched to France to attempt to recover the wreckage. General dissatisfaction was also voiced over the amount of low-level flight training carried out in the area.

A second Hawker Osprey was lost in this area on 3 September 1937. This aircraft was from 801 Squadron and based on HMS *Furious*. It was lost as it attempted to land on the aircraft carrier. Having drifted during a slow approach to the flight deck it made a heavy landing and bounced back into the air. The pilot opened up the throttle to attempt an overshoot but the slow moving machine stalled, hit a 'pom-pom' gun followed by the ship's funnel and radio mast and plunged inverted into the sea with the engine at full throttle. The pilot, Sub-Lt C.A. Knocker, was killed. The aircraft was not recovered from the sea and was struck off charge (SOC) during November 1937.

In response to Air Ministry specification R2/33, Messrs Saunders-Roe (Saro) submitted an innovative design, the Saro A.33. In this machine, the 95ft span wing was mounted 'parasol' fashion above the 75ft long hull, and large tapered sponsons were fitted to the hull sides to provide lateral stability. Powered by four wing-mounted 830hp Bristol Perseus radial engines, heavily armed and able to carry a 2000lb bomb load, the A.33 was a competitor to the ultimate winner of specifica-

Float-equipped Hawker Osprey III. (Air Britain)

Saro A33, serial K4773, under tow following structural failure of wing mounting during take-off on 25 October 1938. (GKN Westland Aerospace)

tion R2/33, the Short Sunderland. The Air Ministry was suitably impressed with the design and test performance data of the proposed A.33 that it issued an order for one prototype (K4773). Taxiing trials commenced on 10 October 1938 and the aircraft made its first flight on 14 October.

Eleven days later, whilst attempting a high speed take-off from the Solent, K4773 passed through the wake of a Red Funnel ferry causing it to porpoise violently, throwing the aircraft prematurely into the air where it stalled badly and crashed back onto the water. The impact caused structural failure of the starboard wing just inboard of the starboard inner engine, the wing twisting forward and forcing the starboard inner propeller into the hull causing a large gash and throwing debris into the tailplane. Fortunately none of the crew was injured and as the damage to the hull was above the water line, the aircraft did not sink. It was towed back to Cowes where it was inspected, but as lengthy and costly repairs would have been needed to return the aircraft to flying condition it was decided that further development should be abandoned, and the Ministry order for a further eleven production machines was cancelled.

February 1939 saw the loss of another sea-going machine when on the 7th, a float equipped Blackburn Shark II, L2384, from No.2 Anti Aircraft Co-operation Unit suffered engine failure and ditched off Eastney. An attempt was made to recover the ditched machine but the Shark sank whilst under tow back to shore.

The last weeks of August 1939 saw a spate of accidents around the Island. This was almost certainly due to the increased amount of training and coastal patrols being carried out in this period before the expected conflict with Germany. The first incident occurred on 14 August and involved another Blackburn Shark II from 2 AACU based at Gosport. This was L2342, which in almost identical conditions to the earlier Shark incident suffered engine failure and capsized during a landing attempt in Stokes Bay, off Gosport. Its pilot P/O P.S.B. Ensor narrowly escaped drowning as the machine turned turtle on impact, initially trapping him in the cockpit before he could free himself from his safety straps and struggle to the surface. He was rescued from the upturned hull by a high speed RAF launch that later returned to salvage his wrecked machine.

Between 21 and 23 August, three further aircraft crashed, two military and one civil, in separate incidents within forty-eight hours; the civil crash producing the only fatality, that of a flying instructor at Lea (Sandown) Airport.

The first of the military aircraft to crash was a Vickers Vildebeast (K4603?) which plunged into the sea about a mile off Bembridge. According to the eye witness report of a Mr Rideout, who watched the incident from the shore, the machine was one of a flight of two aircraft that were flying overhead and on trying to gain altitude the engine appeared to cut out. The pilot dived the aircraft to gain speed and presumably restart the engine, but it nose-dived into the sea.

Saro A33, seen on the slipway following recovery. Note the large gash in the fuselage just behind the beaching gear leg. (GKN Westland Aerospace)

Fortunately, there were several small boats in the area and although the lifeboat maroon was fired, the lifeboat itself was not launched as a rescue was well in hand by the time the crew had assembled.

The first boat on the scene was the *Silver-Lea* owned by a Mr Martin. This was closely followed by Lord Ebblesham's motor yacht, the *Betsy Jane* which had been some 600yds from the scene, containing Lord and Lady Ebblesham and their son and daughter the Hon. Rowland and Janet Blade, who both dived into the sea and assisted with the rescue of the two crew, one of whom was having considerable trouble getting free from his parachute which was dragging him under. The Blades helped to keep the crewmembers afloat until they could be hauled onto the *Silver-Lea* where Lady Ebblesham's second daughter, Mrs Russell, gave first aid to the two crewmen. Neither of the crew was seriously injured, one sustaining a leg injury and the other a wound above one eye. Also involved in the rescue was a launch being sailed by Mr R. Hudson, the Parliamentary Secretary for Overseas Trade. The newspaper report stated that 'Beyond floating debris there was no trace of the machine'.

At about 11.00hrs on Wednesday 23 August, a Fairey Swordfish from the Fleet Air Arm base at Lee-on-Solent force landed on the fore-shore adjacent to Players Copse near Ryde. The pilot, Lt O'Brien, and two observers all escaped without injury. It appears that whilst flying at around 6,000ft a raft that was stowed under one of the wings came out of its container and was blown backwards onto the rudder. In a somewhat indistinct photograph from the *Isle of Wight County Press* of 26 August, the offending raft can be seen still wrapped around the vertical tail surfaces of the Swordfish. As a result of this the pilot was unable to steer the aircraft effectively and decided to force land on the beach. In doing so he was unable to miss the many rocks that occur on this part of the beach and part of the undercarriage was torn away and one wing badly damaged, the machine coming to rest on the waters edge. Territorial soldiers from a nearby camp were summoned to guard the wreckage until the Navy could recover it later that day.

This aircraft is believed to have been L2776, a Swordfish I from 771 Sqdn based at Lee on Solent, which records show as having suffered a minor accident involving a dinghy on this date but do not specify a location.

Endnote

* No further details of this incident or the serial of the aircraft involved have been traced so a definite type cannot be established; however the most prolific Avro biplane in use by the RAF at this time was the Avro 504 in either K or N variants.

** The Right Hon. Sir Philip A.G.D. Sassoon. Bart. PC, CBE, CMG, MP – Chairman of Royal Aero Club of Great Britain (1931).

Chapter Two

Early Hostilities

September 1939 to August 1940

The long forecast conflict with Germany began when war was formally declared on 3 September 1939. Air sorties began almost immediately and the number of aircraft using the airspace around the Island quickly grew.

The war was only sixteen days old before the first wartime victim came to grief when a Fairey Swordfish Mark 1, Serial L2769, from the Gosport-based Torpedo Training Unit (TTU) suffered engine failure whilst formation flying at around 500ft

Avro Anson, Transport and Light Communications Aircraft. (Air Britain)

and was forced to ditch into the sea one mile west of the Nab Tower where it quickly sank. Its pilot, Midshipman J.W. Lowe, was unhurt.

A second Fairey Swordfish suffered a similar fate nine days later when on 26 September, serial number K5983, attached to 'A' flight from the Fleet Air Arm base at Gosport, crashed into the sea five miles south west of Ventnor whilst on a coastal patrol flight. Its pilot, P/O M.F. Llewellyn-Thomas (RAF), was rescued unhurt by the RAFA launch Adastral.

The last loss of 1939 occurred on 20 November and was that of Blackburn Shark III K8898, another Fleet Air Arm aircraft from 2AACU at Gosport. The seaplane suffered engine failure during take off from the sea off Hurst Castle and crashed back into the water. P/O Brand (RAF) was rescued uninjured and the remains of the aircraft were salvaged but were so badly damaged (Cat.W) that the aircraft was SOC a month later.

Six days into the New Year of 1940 the Island's high ground claimed its first wartime victim. This was Avro Anson, serial number K6246 of 48 Squadron based locally at Thorney Island, which flew into St Catherine's Down near the Hermitage, north-west of the village of Whitwell whilst returning from a convoy patrol. Of the crew of four, only one was to survive the impact. Aircraftsman C.M. Ritter, the radio operator, was dragged from the wreckage and given first aid by a local ARP warden before being taken, badly injured, to Ryde hospital. The other three crew men, Flg-Off H.B. Pearson, Flt Sgt F.M. Fennell and Aircraftsman F.M. Rook were all killed instantly. The incident had happened at around midday in conditions of thick fog and low cloud similar to those that claimed the Blackburn Dart in 1926 and was yet to claim further victims.

Fifty-four years later in August 1994, a lady digging in her garden near to the Chequers public house at Rookley unearthed the tail wheel and axle assembly of an aircraft. It was at first assumed that it would have been from Messerschmitt Bf110 U8+HH, which crashed very close to that location in September 1940. However subsequent research via Dunlop Aviation into the part numbers stamped onto the hub show it to be from an Avro Anson.

Only three Ansons are on record as having crashed onto the Island, the other two being a civil conversion which crashed onto St Boniface post war and an RAF machine which force-landed at Somerton and was recovered and repaired. Given that the second incident was during peacetime and the crash would have been investigated by the Civil Aviation Authority who would have collected the wreckage for examination it would seem reasonable to assume that wheel was from the aircraft detailed above. How it came to be in a garden some five miles from the crash site remains unknown.

Almost a month to the day later, on 5 February a Blackburn Shark III, K8934, from the Torpedo Training Unit at Gosport lost its bearings whilst flying without radio in thick local fog and force-landed into the sea off Hillhead and overturned. Its pilot Sqdn Ldr J.V. Hartley was rescued without harm, the aircraft was declared Cat.W.

The next incident occurred approximately three weeks later on 24 February 1940 when a Blackburn Botha 1, (referred to in previous works as a Fleet Air Arm aircraft

Avro Anson tail wheel dug up in a garden near to the Chequers Inn, autumn 1994. Believed to be from K6246 which crashed near the Hermitage, 6 January 1940. (A.T. Gilliam)

but it was in fact an RAF machine) serial no. L6111 from the Torpedo Dropping Unit based at Gosport, on low-level torpedo–dropping exercises at the Stokes Bay ranges suffered an engine failure and flew into the sea off Spit Bank Fort. The pilot Flg-Off Gadd and his crew luckily escaping into their rubber dinghy without injury before the aircraft sank.

The next aircraft to be lost was a Fleet Air Arm machine. This was Fairey Swordfish Mk I, serial L7650, which was lost into the sea off the Needles on 6 March whilst carrying out a mock torpedo attack on HMS *Malahoe*. The aircraft hit the sea during its pull out manoeuvre and fell back into the water where it subsequently sank. Its pilot, Capt. R.H. Parnell (Royal Marines) was uninjured. The machine was declared Cat.C and struck off charge on 1st October 1940

Two days later 22 Sqdn lost Bristol Beaufort I, serial L4475, in an accident when it stalled whilst in the slipstream of another Beaufort and spun into the sea off Hayling Island.

Again a mock attack was to be the cause of the next incident when, on 20 May, two Bristol Blenheim IVs; P4837 & L9455 from 248 Sqdn, were practising an attack on a Bristol Beaufort when they collided, both Blenheims falling into the sea off Thorney Island.

Float equipped Blackburn Shark. (Air Britain)

Blackburn Botha torpedo bomber. (Blackburn Archives)

The coming of summer saw yet another tragedy unfold in the skies over the Island. Just after midnight on the night of the 2/3 of June intense Anti-Aircraft fire was heard, and local search lights were in action although there had been no air raid siren. Shortly afterwards reports were coming in of an aircraft down at Appley near Ryde. Initial excitement at the 'downing' of the Island's first enemy raider soon paled when it was realised that the aircraft was in fact one of ours. The aircraft, a Fairey Battle light bomber, serial no. P2269 from No.12 Operational Training Unit (OTU) based at Andover in Hampshire, crashed onto what is now a playing field at the junction of Puckpool Hill and Appley Road. Two of the crewmembers, Sgt G.H. Hudson and Aircraftsman first class D.L. Leonard, had been killed; the pilot, P/O A.G. Mcintyre, who had parachuted from the aircraft, was injured.

My father told me that he saw the wreckage of this machine in the field close to the main road, albeit covered from prying eyes with large tarpaulins and under a strong military guard, as he passed on his way to work at J.S. White's shipyard early the next morning. He also said that the story circulating at the time was that the flight was unable to deploy the correct 'colour of the day' flare and was therefore fired on by AA batteries on both sides of the Solent, with tragic results.

The field, now used for sport and archery, was at the time two smaller fields with

23

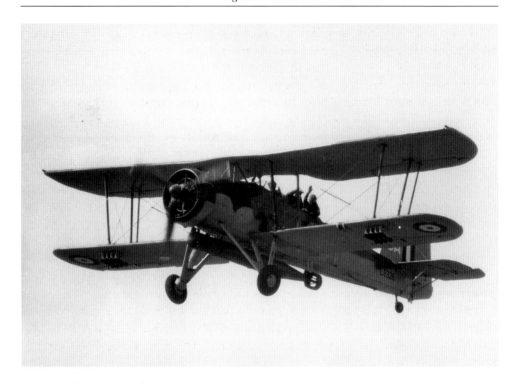

Fairey Swordfish. Naval torpedo attack aircraft. (Air Britain)

a dividing hedge that the aircraft ploughed through before coming to rest. The line of the hedge is shown on old maps and is still easily discernible on site, a shallow depression in the ground indicating the probable impact point.

10 July 1940 saw the 'official' start of the Battle of Britain. The Island's involvement in this epic struggle started one day later on 11 July. Early that morning a Dornier Do 17p of 2(F)11 on a reconnaissance flight was intercepted some twenty miles south of St Catherine's Point by two Hurricanes of 601 Sqdn, based at Tangmere, and shot down into the sea. Its three crewmembers, Lts Vedder, Nest and an unidentified crewman, were all killed.

The day had seen a hectic start to the Island's personal Battle of Britain. Following the downing of the Dornier came a mid-morning raid of Ju87s and Bf110s from Cherbourg against naval targets at Portland, which was intercepted by Hurricanes from several coastal airfields in Hampshire and Dorset.

At 17.15 a large raiding force of Heinkel He111s from 1/KG55 with fighter escort provided by Bf109s was detected by the radar station at Ventnor as it crossed the channel. The raid was intercepted over the north-east of the Island as it approached its Portsmouth target by Tangmere's 601 Sqdn Hurricanes and in the following battle, one Hurricane was hit by return fire from one of the Heinkels. With its gravity fuel tank holed and burning, Flt Sgt A.W. Wooley's Hurricane, P3681, hurtled towards the Island.

Wooley was badly burned and wounded but managed to bale out of his stricken machine and float gently to earth near Thorness Bay whilst his aircraft buried itself in the garden of a house in the small village of Cranmore near Yarmouth.

Forty-two years later this crash was the subject of a 'dig' by aircraft archaeologists who recovered several large pieces of wreckage including the main spar, cockpit area and a remarkably intact Merlin engine. The engine was cleaned and protected against further corrosion and put on display at the then newly opened aviation museum at Tangmere; the very airfield from which it had departed nearly half a century earlier!

At 16.00hrs on Tuesday 16 July, blue section of 601 Squadron, (Flg-Off Rhodes-Moorhouse, Flg-Off Hubbard and P/O Grier) engaged in combat with a Ju88A from 6/KG54 over the Channel near St Catherine's Point. The Junkers, B3+GP plunged into the sea killing Gfr Marb and Ogfr Vetter. The remainder of the crew, Gfr Herbert and F/W Fortmann, were captured.

18 July 1940 saw another 'Friendly Fire' incident, this time involving Spitfire K9990 from 52 Sqdn which was engaged and hit by anti-aircraft fire from a British convoy forcing the pilot to abandon the aircraft off the Island.

Two days later Hurricane I, P3964 from 43 Sqdn was shot down in combat with a Heinkel 115 Air-Sea-Rescue Seaplane south of the Needles at around 18.00hrs. Flg-Off Haworth baled out from the stricken aircraft but despite a long air-sea search, he was never found.

On 21 July another Hurricane I, P3973, from Tangmere-based 43 Squadron was involved in a mid-air collision with a Bf109E-4 from 7/Jg27, five miles south of the Needles. The Hurricane was lost into the sea killing its pilot P/O DeMancha, the enemy aircraft also plunging into the sea taking its pilot Lt Kroker to a watery grave.

In the early afternoon of 25 July, a Messerschmitt Bf109E-4 from Stab III of Jg/27 stalled during an attack on a Hurricane (P/O Goodman) from 1 Sqdn and crashed into the sea ten miles south of St Catherine's Point. The German pilot, Obltn Kirstein, was killed.

West Sussex's Tangmere airfield suffered another loss on 26 July when its 601 Sqdn lost Hurricane MkI, P2753, into the sea south of St Catherine's Point following combat with Obltn Bobislav's Bf109 from III/JG27. Its twenty-year-old pilot, P/O Challoner-Lindsay, was washed ashore and buried at Wimereux in France.

July saw Gosport-based 22 Sqdn undergoing an intensive torpedo course over the Solent. Just prior to their departure to North Coates one of their number suffered a similar fate to that which had befallen the Botha some six months previously. On 1 August a Vickers Vildebeast, serial K6408, hit the sea near Ryde pier whilst on a torpedo dropping exercise. This incident however had a more tragic ending; P/O A. Bailey was killed and his crewman Aircraftsman R.S. Budd was injured.

8 August 1940 was to see the areas greatest number of incidents in single day. A staggering thirty-three aircraft were downed on and around the Island on this day of furious air battles. Of these thirty-three aircraft, all but two ended their days in the sea.

The prime cause of the day's massive tally were the large scale attacks mounted by the Germans on convoy CW9, codename 'Peewit', as it passed along the English Channel to the south of the Island. The convoy had departed from the River

Medway the previous day and had been attacked that night whilst off Dover by a force of E-Boats which had succeeded in sinking three ships and damaging two more. More importantly, the attack had caused the convoy to spread out making defence more difficult. On the morning of 8 August a small force of Ju87 Stukas carried out an attack, losing two of their number and further scattering the convoy in the process.

The second wave of the air attack caught the convoy off the southern coast of the Island. This was a much larger force consisting of fifty-seven Ju87 Stukas accompanied by a large fighter escort. This attack was met by a strong allied fighter defence, which found the slow-flying Stukas an easy target.

I/StG3 suffered three aircraft shot down and one damaged whilst I/StG2 and III/StG2 each had one aircraft badly shot up. A third wave of attackers from 2/StG77 was particularly badly mauled, losing three bombers plus a further five damaged.

A final assault was launched during the afternoon as the convoy passed the back of the Island and ran for shelter towards Weymouth bay by some eighty Stukas with fighter cover being supplied by Bf109s, whilst around seventy Bf110s were used to deal with the convoy's barrage balloon screen and for general 'flak' suppression.

Crashed Ju87, Stuka dive bomber S2+LM pauses en route to the mainland outside the St Lawrence Inn near Ventnor, August 1940. (A. Saunders)

British Armourers remove ammunition from crashed Ju87. This may be the Stuka that crashed at Ventnor. (S2+LM). (IWM neg no.HN88536)

During this attack the Kommandeur of 11/StG77, Hauptman Waldermar Plewig was shot down into the sea to the south-west of the Island by a Hurricane of 145 Sqdn. Plewig was rescued and spent the rest of the war in captivity. He was awarded the Knight's Cross whilst in captivity for his part in the assault, and the decoration was sent from Germany and presented with full honours by the Commander of the POW camp. He was later promoted to Major on 1 April 1942. His crewman, Feldwebel Schover, was killed in the action.

St Lawrence saw the crash landing of Ju87b, unit-marking S2+LM, this aircraft had been attacked by 145 Sqdn Hurricane P3896 which had been scrambled from the West-Sussex airfield of Westhampnett at 16.15hrs Its pilot, P/O P.L. Parrott, attacked the Stuka beam on at an altitude of less than 100ft as it pulled out of its bombing dive and it immediately turned north and ran towards the Island. He continued the attack from astern until the aircraft reached the coast when he ceased firing as the aircraft seemed to be attempting a forced landing. The Stuka came down at The Shute at St Lawrence in a field near the hospital. Despite the battle damage and the fact that the aircraft hit a tree at the end of its landing run it suffered suprisingly little damage, especially as its bomb load was still intact! This was the first Stuka to be captured substantially intact on English soil and was the first enemy aircraft to crash onto the Island. It

P/O John Cruttenden, 43 Sqdn, lost when his Hurricane, P3781, crashed into the sea off St Lawrence. (Cruttenden Family)

was dismantled at the site and taken away by the RAF. Of the crew the pilot, Unteroffizir Schubert, was killed and his crewman, Uffz Pittroff, was taken prisoner.

Meanwhile the battle was developing into a major dogfight spreading over and beyond the Island. Hurricanes of 43 Sqdn and 145 Sqdn from Tangmere and Westhampnett, and 238 Sqdn from Middle Wallop tore into both the dive-bombers and their fighter escorts. Losses were heavy on both sides. Only one other aircraft was to crash onto the Island that day. 43 Sqdn Hurricane P3267 crash-landed at Ford farm near Whitwell. Ventnor ARP reported the aircraft down due to engine failure. P/O H.C. Upton was uninjured.

The RAF's other losses in this action amounted to a further thirteen Hurricanes lost. Of these thirteen aircraft, 43 Sqdn lost two: P3468, piloted by P/O R.S. Oelofse, who was killed when his aircraft crashed into the sea south of Ventnor and P3781 which met a similar fate off St Lawrence also killing its pilot, P/O J. Cruttenden, who had only joined 43 Sqdn in late June. Fresh from an Operational Training Unit; he sadly lacked experience in dog-fighting.

145 Sqdn lost five aircraft: P3545, into the sea south of Ventnor, pilot Sub-Lt F.A. Smith killed; P2955, listed as into sea south-west of Island killing P/O L. Sears;

P2957, listed as into sea south-west of Compton Bay, P/O E. Wakenham killed, and P3163 into sea south of the Needles.

This last mentioned aircraft was piloted by P/O Richard Ughtres Paul Kay Shuttleworth, Second Baron of Gawthorpe, Royal Air Force Volunteer Reserve (RAVR), who was a relative of Richard Ormonde Shuttleworth – another serving RAF officer, who had been killed in a flying accident in Fairey Battle L4971 at Ewelme in Oxfordshire on 2 August. The Shuttleworth family thus lost two of its members within six days. The well-known Shuttleworth aviation collection in Bedfordshire was later founded in honour of R.O. Shuttleworth by his mother. 145 Sqdn's last loss of the day was P3381, Sgt E.D. Baker, which fell to the guns of a Bf109 and plunged into the sea to the south of the Island. Northholt-based 257 Sqdn lost P2981, Flt Lt N.M. Hall, into the sea off St Catherine's Point following action with another Bf109 and reported two further Hurricanes, P3058, Flg-Off D'Arcy-Irvine & R4094, Sgt K.B. Smith, missing following an interception off St Catherine's Point.

238 Sqdn lost the final three aircraft, all listed as crashing into the sea to the south west of the Island. They were: P3823, Flt Lt D. Turner killed; P3617, Flt Lt C. MacCaw killed and another Hurricane from which Sqdn Ldr H. Fenton was rescued. This machine has been referred to in other publications as being P2497. However that serial relates to a Miles Magister that crashed during an aerobatic display on 15 March 1940, it is much more likely that the actual machine that was shot down that day was similarly numbered P2947, a 238 Sqdn aircraft listed as having ditched off the Island following air combat with a He59 whilst on convoy escort duties that day.

The Germans fared worse still. In addition to the two incidents already described, a further seventeen aircraft fell into the sea around the Island. From the dive-bomber group six Ju87s were lost as follows: One from 3/stg3, south of Ventnor, Uffz Walz and Gefr Shutz killed; two aircraft from 2/stg3 south of the Island, Fws Zechweiger and Heinrick killed and from the second machine Uffzs Kleinhans and Quante were listed as missing; one aircraft from 4/stg77 to the south of the Island, Hpt Schmarck and Gefr Wuttle killed; 1/stg3 lost one aircraft off Brighstone killing Obltn Muller and Uffz Krampfl and 1/stg77 a further machine off Blackgang, its crew of Hptm Plegeg and an unidentified crewman also lost their lives.

The fighter escort was also badly mauled, losing eleven aircraft. Two Bf110C4s from unit V/LG1 went into the sea to the south west of the Needles, of the two crews three men were listed as killed and one as missing. Unit 9/JG27 lost two Bf109Es, one south of Ventnor from which the pilot baled out and was rescued and the other south of the Needles from which Uffz L. Girbach was rescued wounded. Unit 2/JG7 lost four Bf109Es including that of its Kommodore, Hptm W. Andres who was rescued from the sea to the south west of Ventnor; F/W E. Rencke (Krenzke?) was shot down and rescued south west of St Catherine's Point as was Uffz Uebe; Uffz Schultz was killed when his fighter plunged into the sea off Brook. Unit 1/JG27 lost two aircraft and pilots, Lts L. Birkenbach and K. Bothfield died when their aircraft went into the sea at Atherfield and Monks Bay respectively.

During the course of this action German air-sea rescue services were in action with both high speed launches and Heinkel He59 seaplanes and many of the rescued

Blackburn Roc 1, Fleet Air Arm fighter/target tug aircraft. (Blackburn Archives)

German pilots were picked up by one or other of these. The last of the German losses was to come from the air sea rescue forces, Seenotflug KDO losing a He59 into the sea south of St Catherine's Point, its entire crew listed as missing.

The convoy suffered no further attacks but it had been badly mauled. Only four ships out of its original total remained unscathed.

Three days later, on 11 August, the Luftwaffe attacked in force again. This time the main target was to be Portland Naval base, with a secondary attack on Weymouth. A large force of bombers with fighter escort was detected by Ventnor radar station and Spitfires and Hurricanes were scrambled from Nos 1, 87, 145, 213, 238, 601 & 609 Squadrons. Interception took place over the western end of the Island and a vicious dogfight took place, which saw five aircraft down, in this area.

Hurricane V7294 of No.145 Squadron at Tangmere went down into the sea to the south of the Needles, its pilot, Flg-Off Oestowiez was reported missing. Also from 145 Squadron, Hurricane P3164 crash-landed at Mottistone, 300 yards south of Mottistone Manor. Flown by Sqdn Ldr J. Peel, who shared, along with Sqdn Ldr Fenton (P2947), shot down during the convoy defence on 8 August, the distinction of being the highest ranking British pilots to be shot down over the Island. He was slightly injured in the crash, and was attended to in the wartime manner with a customary stiff drink supplied by the owner of Mottistone Manor, the first Lord Mottistone (Lord Lieutenant of Hampshire and the Isle of Wight).

Another Tangmere loss on this day was Hurricane P3172 from No.1 Sqdn flown by P/O J.A.J. Davey, which crashed at the site of what is now Sandown High School. The aircraft had been damaged following combat with a Bf110 and crashed whilst attempting a wheels down landing on the football pitch. The incident was witnessed by several people. One account was given to me by Mr A. Smith, who as a young boy lived only minutes away from the site. He recounted that the aircraft made a satis-factory touch-down but could not stop before impacting with a hedgerow. As was common in those days the hedge contained a raised earth bank, which caused the aircraft to come to an abrupt halt and to tip onto its nose. Mr Smith remembers that the pilot threw his identity tag clear of the aircraft but within seconds the fuel tank in one wing exploded and the wreckage was engulfed in flames. There was no hope of the pilot being saved and so with stray ammunition from the burning wreckage beginning to fly dangerously around, Mr Smith returned home.

A second, and differing, account was related by another witness. He vividly remembered the day when, as a lad of six years, he was blackberrying in the field with his sister as the tragedy unfolded.

He remembered seeing the Hurricane descending trailing smoke, and related the following tale:

'I was standing by the hedge as the plane made its landing, the Hurricane looked gigantic to me at the time and I was very scared. The pilot saw me and braked hard, this caused the tail of the aircraft to go up. The nose of the aircraft dug into the ground as it came to a halt. I saw the pilot trying to open the cockpit canopy. I remember seeing the pilot heaving at the canopy with his feet on the instrument panel to get more leverage. Suddenly blue flames spurted from the engine compartment. The flames were fierce, like a blowlamp. They rapidly engulfed the cockpit. I heard a sound, which reminded me of the hiss from a bicycle pump. This was the sound of bullets spraying around me. My sister was screaming at me to lie down but I decided to get up and run for safety. I am convinced that the pilot died trying to save me. If he had gone through the hedge the plane would have halted safely and he would probably have been able to escape.'

Fifty-three years to the day later, a memorial to this event was unveiled close to the site of the crash. The memorial service was attended by several eyewitnesses of the crash, as well as local residents and representatives of several service organisations.

P/O Davey was laid to rest a short distance from the crash site at Sandown cemetery, his service headstone recording his age as a mere twenty years. He is the only Battle of Britain pilot shot down over the Island to be buried locally.

German losses amounted to two Bf109Es from jg.27. Uffz S. Lackner was reported as missing when his machine plunged into the sea south west of the Needles, whilst Obltn H. Fricke was killed when his machine went into the sea south-west of the Island.

Messerschmitt Bf109E, seen on display following crash-landing. It is believed that this is Grey 2, piloted by Feldwebel C. Hansen, which force-landed at Bathingbourne on 16 August 1940.
(By courtesy of the Portsmouth Evening News)

12 August saw another large German attack on the area, when 200 aircraft were approaching from the Cherbourg area. Whilst the main attack was destined to be for Portsmouth, secondary targets included airfields in Sussex and Kent and also the Chain Home radar station on the down above Ventnor. This attack carried out by Ju88s from KG51 resulted in considerable damage to the radar station, which was rendered inoperable for several days. Air losses were again high on both sides, a total of fourteen aircraft crashing in the area.

One of the early casualties of this conflict was Mk I Spitfire N3175 from 266 Sqdn, based at Tangmere. This was reported as shot down near Portsmouth at 12.18hrs, it was in fact severely damaged and attempted a forced landing at Bembridge Airport. P/O W.S. Williams was unhurt and able to scramble clear before the aircraft was totally destroyed by fire. 266 Sqdn also lost another Mk I Spitfire, serial P9333, into the sea off Portsmouth in this action. One report shows that the body of the unfortunate P/O D.G. Ashton was recovered but then re-buried at sea.

Warmwell's 152 Sqdn lost two Spitfires, both Mk Is, P9456 crashed into the sea to the south-west of Ventnor following combat with a Ju88. Its pilot Flt Lt L.C. Withall was posted as missing in action; whilst K9999 crashed into the sea off St Catherine's Point, killing its pilot P/O D.C. Shepley after tangling with another Ju88.

145 Sqdn based at Tangmere's satellite field at Westhampnett lost four Hurricanes in this area. All four fell into the sea around the Island, P3736 piloted by Flt Lt Boyd and R4176 piloted by Flg-Off W. Pankratz to the south of the Island and R4180 to the south of Ventnor. Its pilot, P/O H. Harrison was killed, as were the other two. The fourth machine P3391, piloted by Sgt J. Kwiecinski, was also lost into the sea to the south of the Island.

The last allied loss of the day was Hurricane P3662 from 257 Sqdn at Northolt. This was lost into the sea at Spithead, its pilot P/O J.A.G. Chomley being posted as missing.

Enemy losses amounted to five Ju88s from unit KG51 and one Bf110 from 2ZG/2. Of these, all but one aircraft ended up in the sea. These were Ju88 serial 9K+F2 from 3/KG51 reported as lost south of Portsmouth (presumably in the sea off Ryde) with the loss of crew members Obltns Wildernuth & Stern, Gefr Dreese and Uffz Rosch. Ju88 from 3/KG51 with the loss of Obltn Schlegal and three other unknown crew; Ju88 from 6/KG51 with the loss of Obltn Flegal, Uffz Bergkammer, Gefrs Rener & Rucket; Ju88 from 8/KG51 with the loss of Ltn Seidel, Obfw Lukoschars, Sdfhr Bigalke and Uffz Fischer, who were all reported as lost in sea off the Island.

Messerschmitt Bf110 from 2/ZG2 crashed into the Spithead near Ryde with the loss of Uffz Budig and Hptm Kulbel. The Squadron Commander of 213 Sqdn, Hector McGregor, got his Hurricane onto the tail of this Bf110 and with one burst of machine gun fire sent it into the sea off Forelands. The crew of two perished in the sea, which by a strange quirk of tide and current washed the body of Fritz Budig ashore at Gosport whilst Kulbel's body was found five weeks later on the beach near Boulogne.

The last of the day's Ju88 crashes was that of 9K+AA from Stab. KG51 (head-quarters flight). This aircraft was piloted by the Kommodore of KG51, Oberst Dr Fisser, who was the highest ranking German to be shot down on the Island. Fisser led his unit on a course parallel to the Sussex coast and some fifteen miles offshore. As the Isle of Wight came into view he maintained a westerly course up the Solent in a bid to convince the defending forces that his unit was repeating the previous days raid on Portland. As the force approached Portsmouth Fisser turned a section of his unit south-west and descended. Racing over Forelands point (Bembridge) at 5,000ft and 300mph they headed for Ventnor where on the high ground above the town stood the Chain Home radar towers. Fisser's preferred tactic was a shallow dive attack, which gave his bomb aimer more time to make last minute adjustments than the traditional 45 degree dive bomb attack. After release of the four 250kg bombs his trajectory took him down over the town and out to sea, behind him was the badly damaged radar station.

Immediately after the attack, Fisser ordered his unit to close up and climb to make good their escape. At this point, he realised that his unit was in a dangerous situation. His unit would gain only limited protection from the few Bf110s that were flying defensive cover in his area and following the diving attack he now also clearly had a height disadvantage.

Hurricanes from 213 and Spitfires from 152 Sqdns were on them before they could clear the area. Fisser's Ju88 was attacked by a Hurricane from 213 Sqdn and came down south of Godshill at Bridgecourt farm at 12.25hrs. The aircraft burst into flames following the crash as the crew scrambled clear. Obltn Luderitz, Lt Schad, Sdfhr Northelfer survived to spend the rest of the war as POWs. Dr Fisser was not so fortunate, he was reported to have climbed from the cockpit with his clothes on fire, falling into a nearby hedge, which also caught fire. An army Colonel and his driver tended his injuries as best they could but despite their efforts, the Oberst died shortly after the crash.

In his book, *Battle in the Skies*, H.J.T. Leal shows a photograph recorded as from a Swedish air historian of a Ju88 believed to 9K+AA on display at Stirling in Scotland in aid of Stirling's Spitfire fund. Whilst the aircraft in this photo undoubtedly displays the code letter A, it does not seem to be as significantly damaged or burnt as the crash reports indicate it should be, so some doubt must be placed upon the credibility of this photo.

13 August saw 238 Sqdn lose another Hurricane I to the guns of a Messerschmitt Bf109 when P3764 was shot down into the sea to the south of the Island. Its pilot, Sgt Seabourne, was rescued from the sea suffering from burns.

In addition, Sgt J. Hallowes of 43 Sqdn claimed to have shot down a Ju88, which crashed in flames into a wood at Thorness Bay. No other source lists this incident.

14 August brought further raids on this area but on a smaller scale. Heinkel He111s attacking Southampton and Middle Wallop. One He111 from 3/KG27 was lost into the sea south west of the Needles, its crew comprising Lt Uhland and four others were reported as missing. Alternative sources list this machine as having crashed at Canns Farm, Puriton in Somerset.

Five German aircraft were shot down the next day, 15 August. The first aircraft lost was a Dornier Do17p from unit 3(F) 31 based at Nantes, intercepted just after dawn whilst on a reconnaissance flight by Spitfires from 213 Squadron, it was shot down into the sea to the south of Ventnor. Its crew, consisting of Lt Raasch, Obltn Horn and Gefr Grupp were all killed. During the afternoon a large raiding force of Ju88s escorted by Bf110s crossed the Island en-route to Middle Wallop airfield in Hampshire, recrossing the Island on its return to France. The raid was intercepted by Spitfires from 609 and 234 Sqdns. Four Bf110s were claimed shot down in this area. The first was from 7/ZG76 and fell into the sea to the south of the Island taking its crew of Uffz Haas and Gefr Hoffman with it.

The second Bf110, MB+BP, was attacked as it was returning from this raid by two Polish pilots, Flg-Off Ostraszewski from 609 Sqdn and P/O Janusz Zurakowski from 234 Sqdn both being accredited with a 'half kill'. The Bf110 from 2/ZG76 based at Rennes and carrying marking MB+BP and the distinctive Sharks Teeth nose art of the 'Haifisch' (Shark) geschwader is recorded as having crashed at 18.06hrs at West Ashey farm. The machine had roared in low from the north of the Island, passing low enough over Wooton hill for bus passengers, who had followed the normal practise of vacating the bus during an air raid and taking whatever cover they could find, to look up and clearly see the rear gunner.

The aircraft was first hit as it flew over the Solent causing the starboard engine to burst into flames. Further hits stopped the port engine and wounded the pilot, Uffz Guscheweski, rendering him unconscious. He came to around the time that the plane crash-landed but could not move as a result of his injuries. The rear gunner, F/W Bindorfer, died from bullet wounds received at the crash site following the arrival of troops from a Scottish infantry regiment who were billeted at nearby Havenstreet.

Various reasons have been given for his being shot. Adrian Searle in his book *The Island At War* quotes a Mr Vernon Scambell who claimed that Bindorfer fired on the soldiers as they approached the plane, the soldiers returned fire, raking the plane from end to end with machine gun fire from a Vickers machine gun positioned on the road above. Given the approximately north/south direction of travel of the aircraft it should have force-landed with its nose roughly towards the downs and the road leading up to it. The crash site was described to me as adjacent to the corner of the hedge in the first field past West Ashey farm (map ref. 574882). If this is the case, it is difficult to believe that Bindorfer's gun could have been trained either on soldiers approaching from the road or upon the soldiers manning the Vickers machine gun on the road above the crash site.

The Ryde ARP authorities reported briefly that 'one of the crew had been shot by the military as he was interfering with the controls (of the aircraft) and would not desist.' My father's recollection of the incident was that Bindorfer was shot whilst resisting capture.

Bindorfer was the first and indeed the only German service man to be shot on the Island. The pilot fared better. He was released from the aircraft by the soldiers. His injuries were such that he could not stand, his left side being paralysed. Whilst he was laid on the grass his recollections were that the soldiers, particularly the officer in charge, showed him great kindness. He was removed first to a police cell for the night and then later to Parkhurst military hospital where his back and head injuries were operated on. Guscheweski spent the rest of the war as a prisoner of war.

The crashed aircraft drew several sightseers from the local area, one of whom, a then eleven-year-old Mr Williams from Haylands, was suprised to find that one of the Black Watch soldiers guarding the wreckage was his brother-in-law. Mr Williams recalled that the aircraft was substantially intact although a little souvenir hunting had taken place, including the removal by his brother-in-law of what Mr Williams describes as a black clock-shaped instrument.

P/O Zurakowski who was part credited with this event was himself shot down over the Island nine days later.

The third Bf110 was a C variant from 6/Zg76, MB+WP, which failed to return to its base and is believed to have fallen into the sea following combat off the Island. The crew of F/W Wagner and Uffz Sporl were recorded as missing. The final German Bf110 loss of the day was from 7/Zg76 that was shot down into the sea south of the Island. Again, the crew, Uffzs Kschamer and Voight, were posted as missing.

Friday 16 August brought renewed attacks on south coast targets by the Luftwaffe. The brunt of these attacks were focused on the airfields at Lee-on-Solent, Gosport and Tangmere, whilst around half a dozen Ju87s dive bombed the already damaged radar station at Ventnor, delaying its return to service until late September. Sporadic attacks continued across the Island for the remainder of the day and five aircraft were shot down as a result.

The RAF lost two fighters; Flg-Off C.A. Woods-Scawen was slightly injured when his 43 Sqdn Hurricane, N3251, crashed in flames at Horsebridge Hill on the outskirts of Newport at around 13.40hrs. Woods-Scawen, who had been previously shot down in R4102 only three days earlier, was one of two RAF pilot brothers: Flg-Off P.P. Woods-Scawen from 85 Sqdn was killed in action on 1 September 1940; C.A. Woods-Scawen's Hurricane came down at or very near to what is now the Agricultural Show Ground. One eye witness report of the time from a passenger on a passing Cowes to Newport bus remembered seeing just the tailplane sticking out of a hole in the field. Whilst another remembered seeing a substantially undamaged Hurricane on the ground opposite Parkhurst Barracks on the day after. Despite searches in the area by modern day aircraft enthusiasts no wreckage of this aircraft has yet been discovered.

Around teatime Flg-Off H.P. Connor from 234 Sqdn was fished uninjured from the sea near Bonchurch by an Air Sea Rescue launch. He had baled out of his Mk I Spitfire X4016 following an encounter with a Messerschmitt Bf109, the stricken aircraft crashing in flames a quarter of a mile north of The Heights, on the Whitwell road out of Ventnor.

German losses amounted to three aircraft, one of which became probably the most publicly inspected enemy aircraft to have crashed in the area. Bf109E, Grey2+, from 2/JG53 based at Rennes in France, was intercepted by Spitfires of 234 Sqdn and came down at Bathingbourne Farm, to the south-west of the main Sandown to Newport road midway between Apse Heath and the Fighting Cocks public house.

Its pilot, F/W Christian Hansen, suffered no serious injuries and surrendered to some local farm workers who detained him until the arrival of the local Arreton War Reserve Constable where upon he was arrested and transported into custody at Newport, after first being allowed to recover from his state of shock over a drink in the nearby Fighting Cocks!

His fighter was only slightly damaged and official permission was gained for the Fire service to temporarily recover the machine back to their Newport headquarters where it was put on display. The local Spitfire Fund★ benefited from this display. Local people were only too happy to pay the sum of sixpence to sit in the cockpit of one of the enemy's premier fighter aircraft. An enterprising local printer produced mock 'In Memorium' cards which he sold for three-pence to further boost the fund.

The other two German losses that day were a Bf109 from 3/JG53 which crashed into the sea, its pilot F/W Dinger was rescued, and a Heinkel HE111P from 1/KG27 whose crew were rescued from the sea to the south-east of the Island by the German air-sea rescue service.

By comparison to the previous days, 17 September was a quiet day. The sole loss in this area appears to be that of Bristol Blenheim L4833 from 235 Sqdn which crashed into the sea as it made a night approach to the airfield at Thorney Island following a mission escorting Fairey Battles to and from Bolougne.

Following a day's respite, the aerial battles resumed their destruction on 18 September with a total of ten aircraft reported down in this area following attacks on the airfields at Thorney Island, Lee-on-Solent, Gosport and the radar installation at Poling in Sussex.

One of the first casualties of the day was reported around 14.30hrs when a Ju87 from 2/StG77 based at Cannes apparently failed to recover from a dive bombing attack and struck the sea about a mile off Dunnose Head at Ventnor carrying its crew of Obltn Morenski and an unnamed crew man to a watery grave.

Around half an hour later Obltn R. Moeller-Friedrich's Bf109E-4 from 6/JG27 smashed into the ground at Tapnell farm, Afton near Freshwater. The pilot baled out successfully, floating down onto St Martin's Down, Wroxall, to be taken prisoner by a detachment of troops who were exercising in the area. This wreck was subsequently dug in 1982. As the aircraft had only partially buried itself in the crash and the bulk of the wreckage had been removed at the time, only the propeller hub and reduction gear and a few fragments of engine were found. An extract from an official crash listing of the time reports that the aircraft was completely wrecked. Markings were indiscernible but the nameplate on a tailplane rib carried the following information: Weserflugzeugbau: Serial 22301/225, Zeichen 109-36-00, Fabrik Monat 10/39.

Several other Bf109s from this same unit were also shot down. 'Yellow 6+', piloted by Lt Julius Neumann took a direct hit from behind which destroyed his cooling system and left him no option but to attempt a forced landing on St Martin's Down, east of Wroxall. The crash-landing left Neumann, who would celebrate his twenty-fifth birthday the next day, unhurt and he surrendered to two Home Guard soldiers who had arrived breathless at the crash site. After ensuring that the pilot had no weapon on him, they enquired if he had any 'souvenirs'. Neumann replied that he had not come to England to distribute souvenirs! He did have a pair of Luftwaffe issue sunglasses, so he broke them in halves and gave half to each of the soldiers who seemed delighted with their trophies. The pilot accredited with shooting down Neumann was Sqdn Ldr H.J.L. 'Jim' Hallowes of 43 Sqdn. Many years after the war Neumann and Hallowes were put in contact with each other by historian Alfred Price and the two men became firm friends.

An official crash report of the time categorised the machine as a Bf109D and reported that it had landed on fire following fighter action. The engine, cockpit and starboard wing had burnt out, the pilot's instruments were destroyed but the 'wireless' in the fuselage was intact and set to a frequency of twenty-four megacycles. It went on to state that the aircraft carried the markings '6+—' (horizontal line); the six and horizontal lines outlined in black. Its Werknummer was 1455.

Fifty-four years later Herr Neumann returned to the Island as a result of correspondence and research by a local Shanklin man, and visited the scene of his wartime crash where he was able to pinpoint the actual site. Neumann, an experienced pilot with in excess of 170 missions to his credit spent the rest of the war as a POW before returning to Germany where he later rejoined the Luftwaffe as an attaché, before rising through the rank of Station Commander to retire as a Colonel.

Another of the unit's victim was Uffz K. Nolte who was killed when his Bf109 plunged into the sea to the south of the Island, Lt Gerhard Mittsdorfer from 1/JG27 was rescued by a local boat after his Bf109, White 6 +, was shot down into the sea off Monks Bay near Ventnor, whilst Obltn Trumplemann of 7/JG27 was killed when his Bf109 crashed into the sea at Sandown Bay. Farther round the coast at Ryde F/W E. Swallisch from 2/JG27 drowned following the crash of his Bf109 into the sea at Spithead. The last of JG2's losses was that of Obltn Muller who was lost into the sea to the south of the Island.

Two further Ju87 Stuka losses were reported that day, that of Uffzs. Weniger and Mobes from 1/stg.77 who were killed when their machine plunged into the sea near the Nab Tower off Bembridge and also that of Obltn Sonntag and one other unnamed crewman lost into the sea to the south of the Island.

The RAF's losses in this area were considerably lower with only two aircraft down. The first loss being that of Spitfire Mk I, X4110, from 602 Sqdn after tangling with a Messerschmitt 109. Details of this aircraft and its fate vary: one source lists the aircraft as having had its first flight on 7 August and subsequently arriving with 602 Sqdn from 9 Maintenance unit two days before this incident (16 August). This report lists X4110 as shot down by the Bf109 into the Solent, with its injured pilot Flg-Lt Dunlop Urie abandoning the aircraft. Another source states that the aircraft arrived at 602's Westhampnett base on 18 August and it was being scrambled almost immediately, before there was even time to paint on the unit's identification markings, and that following the air battle Urie, despite shell-splinter injuries to his feet, brought the badly damaged machine back to base. A photo accompanying this report shows what appears to be a bullet-ridden X4110, carrying no unit markings; parked at an airfield. Both reports confirm that the aircraft never flew again. One source details the aircraft as SOC on 5 October 1940, the other suggests that this Spitfire probably had the dubious honour of having the shortest service life of any Spitfire, a mere fifteen minutes!

The second loss was that of Hurricane I, P3310, from 151 Sqdn, which was damaged by return fire from a flight of Dornier Do17s and was abandoned over Christchurch Bay.

The 19 August saw a raid on Southampton docks carried out by around 30 Junkers Ju88s of 3KG51 with a fighter escort of Bf109s. One of the Ju88s, an A-1 variant, serial 9K+FR, was shot down into the sea off Ryde, its crew of F/Ws Haak, Moser, Schachtner and Uffz Bachauer were posted as missing. It was this aircraft I believe that my uncle, Mr Sid Gilliam from Nettlestone, used to walk out to at the lowest tides of the year in order to catch lobsters from within its wreckage. Its position was between Ryde pier and Appley beach. During the sixties an inaugural hovercraft service was operated between Appley beach and Southsea and also Gosport using a Westland SRN2 craft. As there was nowhere secure to leave the hovercraft at Appley overnight it was taken back to Westland's factory at East Cowes every night, returning each morning to commence service. On a number of occasions the hovercraft became snared on the wreckage that protruded above the surface at low tides as it travelled on a line from Ryde pier head and Appley beach during its morning journey from Cowes. This being before the days of aircraft archaeology or recovery, the problem was resolved by declaring the wreckage a hazard to navigation and having it blown up; thus removing an obstruction for the hovercraft and also a handy supply of sea food for my uncle!

This Ju88 was accredited to Spitfire Mk I R6703 from 92 Sqdn. The aircraft flown by P/O Wade was hit by return fire from the German bomber over the Solent and exploded after crash landing at Selsey. P/O Wade was listed as safe following the crash.

Three Ju88s were lost the next day as aircraft transited to and from several raids. The Junkers were generally flying singly following small-scale raids; the first to fall was shot down into the Western Solent by a Spitfire from 152 Sqdn. This was M7+EH from 3/KG51 its crew of Uffzs Dressen and Weigand, Obfwl. Sewade and Gefr Springfield were listed as missing.

2/KG54 lost the other two aircraft. The first piloted by Lt Keller, who along with his three crew were lost into the sea to the south west of the Island and that of Lt Mainwold and his crew who entered the sea twenty miles south of the Island.

Previous works have suggested that yet another Ju88 was lost the following day, 22 August. They list unit 3(F)121 as losing an aircraft into the sea to the south-west of the Island, with crew Lt Baudier and two other crewmen listed as missing with one other crew member listed as killed. However, this crew roster was from Ju88a-1, 7A+AL, which although engaged by fighters over the Island, actually crash-landed at Uplott Farm, Beaford, Near Okehampton. Unit 8/KG30 lost a Ju88A-1 from a mission over southern England that day. Hptm. Mainwald and two other NCOs listed as missing. This may have been the aircraft in question.

The destruction of Ju88s went on the next day, following raids on Thorney Island, Tangmere and Portsmouth, with the loss of 9/LG1's ObF/W Ripper, F/W Hoffman and Gefr Shultz when their aircraft slipped below the waves in the sea to the south west of the Needles.

On 24 August Ju88s were indirectly responsible for the loss of an RAF Blenheim 1f light bomber. The machine, T1804, was one of a formation of three aircraft from 235 Sqdn from Thorney Island who were patrolling over the Solent when they were mistaken for the similar looking Ju88s and attacked by Hurricanes of No.1 (RCAF) Sqdn. The aircraft was destroyed before the mistake was realised. T1804 crashed into Bracklesham Bay, taking P/O D.N. Woodger and Sgt D.L. Wright with it. The other two Blenheims, Z5736 & N3351, collided and were damaged. Yet again another tragic incident of 'Friendly Fire' resulted in the loss of an aircraft.

In fact, 24 August was to see a reversal of fortunes in the local air war. Total air losses for the day in and around the area amounting to four allied aircraft for the loss of one German fighter. In addition to the Blenheim, three Spitfires were lost; N3239, a Mk I from 234 Sqdn based at Middle Wallop, crashed at Little Budbridge farm near Godshill following a dogfight with a Bf109. Its pilot was P/O J. Zurakowski who baled out successfully, sustaining only minor injuries. Zurakowski was one of the two pilots accredited with the shooting down of the Bf110 at nearby Ashey nine days earlier in which the unfortunate Bindorfer was shot by troops. The Spitfire was sufficiently damaged to be classified irreparable and was officially SOC on 1 October, Zurakowski survived the war and went on to become a test pilot for Gloster aircraft.

A second Spitfire crashed in the west Wight. This was a Mk I serial L1082 from 609 Sqdn. It had been involved in an engagement with a Bf110 over the Ryde area and came down at Tapnell Farm, near Freshwater. P/O A. 'Andy' Mamedoff, an American Volunteer pilot, is listed in some reports as having baled out and escaped without injury and in others of having successfully force landed the aircraft. The Spitfire could not have suffered too much damage as records show that it was re-issued to No.58 Operational Training Unit (OTU) three months later on 29 January 1941 only to become a total wreck following a flying accident almost exactly a year later on 22 August 1941. It was finally SOC on 2 September 1941.

The identity of the third Spitfire has not been traced. It was recorded as crashing at Broad Lane, Thorley. As Thorley and Tapnell farm are very close together, it may well be that this incident and that of L1082 are in fact the same aircraft. As an interesting aside to this incident, a former Wellow resident, Mr G. Foskett, told me that he clearly remembered a Spitfire making a wheels-up landing at Broad lane. Mr Foskett even indicating the spot to me, but assuring me that this could not have been until 1943 at the earliest.

The single German loss was that of a Bf109e of 6/JG2 and was to prove perhaps one of the more bizarre crashes to take place in the area. The pilot was F/W Gerhardt Ebus. His Messerschmitt was attacked by a Hurricane from 238 Sqdn piloted by P/O W. Gordon and critically damaged. Ebus baled out and seeing that he was drifting out over the sea kicked off his heavy flying boots to increase his chances of survival. The boots having come to earth at two separate locations in Shanklin were rapidly carried off as prized trophies. One became the centrepiece on the consulting room table at a local doctors surgery for many years after the war, the other was apparently displayed in the window of a confectioners shop.

Ebus came down in the sea off Dunnose and had difficulty releasing his parachute. Local longshoremen were at first apparently reluctant to launch a boat to rescue the pilot. When a local boat with a military presence on board finally located him, he had unfortunately drowned. Meanwhile his stricken aircraft had fallen to earth in Greatwoods Copse at Cowlease hill, on the outskirts of Shanklin, amazingly plummeting straight down a boarded-over well, the location of which had been lost for years and had been the subject of several fruitless searches prior to this event.

The fuselage and engine had disappeared completely down the well leaving parts of the wings and tail strewn around the area and large amounts of cannon shells peppered into the trees. The majority of the wreckage was removed from the site at the time.

Around forty years later after much searching for the site an aircraft recovery group carried out a detailed search at the site and recovered several parts of this aircraft including a cannon.

Sunday 25 August saw a morning attack by approximately 150 aircraft on Portland Naval base and Warmwell air base. The attack was met by a spirited defence by aircraft from the airfields at Exeter, Tangmere, Middle Wallop and Warmwell itself. Later that day there was an evening raid on the Portsmouth area. From these raids, five German aircraft were lost. Two Bf110-C4s were lost into the sea off Portsmouth, one of these was crewed by 1/ZG2s Lt Wetsphal and one other unnamed crewman who were reported as killed, and the other from 5/LG1 contained Obltn Glienke and Uffz Stack, this crew was reported as missing. A further Bf110C4 was lost into the sea to the south west of the Needles. Its unidentified crew from 3/ZG26 was rescued by the German air sea rescue service, Seenotflug KDO.

3/JG2 provided fighter cover for the raid and lost two of their aircraft in this area. The Bf109Es came down in the sea to the south and south east of the Island and of their pilots, both of whom are untraced; one was rescued, the other pilot was less fortunate.

The month of August's last losses occurred on the 26th following heavy attacks on Portsmouth and Southampton by Heinkel HE111s from KG55 with supporting fighter cover provided by Bf110s and 109s. Again, effective fighter interception caused losses amongst the German forces. Several Heinkels were shot down, one crashing in this area. This was HE111 G1+GN, from unit 5/KG55, that crashed into the sea off Hanover Point at Brook on the southern coast of the Island. Its crew consisting of Lt Brünning (pilot), Lt Von der Hagen, Uffzs Stieger and Losch and Gefr Stratman were successfully rescued by a German air sea rescue launch.

Also lost that day was a Heinkel HE59 Seaplane operated by Seenotflug KD/02 on air sea rescue duty. Its crew of Lt Mietlin and two other crewmen were killed when it crashed into the sea to the south of the Nab tower lighthouse off Bembridge.

Endnote

* Spitfire Funds raised money from local fund raising schemes towards the cost of a Spitfire; should an individual fund raise enough money to cover the cost of one complete Spitfire that machine became a 'Presentation Aircraft' and was named in honour of the fundraiser. The *Isle of Wight County Press* of 27 September 1941 proudly displayed a photograph of such a Spitfire bearing the name *Vectis*.

Chapter Three

The Battle Continues

September 1940 to October 1940

September 1940 saw the continuation of the Battle of Britain in the skies over the Island. Although the large raids were beginning to scale down there were still to be considerable aircraft losses in this area.

The month was only two days old when the first victim was to fall. Sqdn Ldr P.E. Meagher, from the Special Duties Flight (SDF) from RAF Christchurch, flying Mk I Hurricane L1562, had scrambled following the sounding of an air raid warning. He sighted an enemy aircraft that he believed to be a Dornier 215 out to sea and closed on it, shooting it down into the sea ten miles south-west of the Needles. Observation posts and anti-aircraft gunners on the Island confirmed the victory. However, due to bad aircraft recognition and the fact that as SDF units were not 'official' fighter command units, records have not generally been cross-referenced, there is some doubt as to the actual type of aircraft shot down. The claimed Do215 may have in fact been Ju88, F6+DK from unit 2(f)/122, which was recorded as an unclaimed loss on that day. The crew roster for this aircraft consisted of Obltn Schmidt, F/W Jahnke, Obgfr Rockstrol and Gfr Kronberg.

On 19 September, the same Hurricane was involved in another shoot down. This time the identity of the aircraft was not in doubt. Junkers Ju88, serial 9K+DL, from 1/Kg51 and involved in a raid on Yeovil, was shot down into the sea ten miles to the south of St Catherine's Point. Its crew, comprising of Obfw Luckhart, Uffz Menker, F/W Walter and Gefr Roeder, were killed. The Hurricane was damaged by return fire from the Ju88 but made a safe return to base and was transferred to 50 Maintenance Unit (MU) at Oxford for repairs six days later.

Six days later, 59 Sqdn lost a Bristol Blenheim IV, serial L8793. The aircraft was returning from a Reconnaissance mission when it stalled on approach to Thorney Island and crashed into the sea.

26 September 1940 saw a large raid carried out on the Vickers Supermarine aircraft factory at Woolston, Southampton, by He111s from KG55 escorted by around a hundred Bf110s to provide fighter cover. The raid was successful, the factory was extensively damaged. Losses were again high: nine aircraft are recorded as lost in this area.

Middle Wallop-based 238 Sqdn lost two Hurricanes during this engagement. P3830 crashed onto Merlin's Farm, near to the Sun Inn at Calbourne, missing a telephone box by just a few feet. Its pilot, P/O R.A. Kings, baled out safely. A team of aircraft recovery enthusiasts visited the site in 1982 to find that the site had been partially built on; a milking parlour now covers most of the crash site. A small-scale hand dig was attempted on the small area left uncovered and revealed a smashed engine and a few pieces of cockpit equipment. 238's second loss was that of P3098, which plunged into the sea to the south-west of the Island. Its pilot, Flt Sgt V. Horsky, was posted as missing.

Hurricane P5205, from 607 Sqdn at Tangmere, crashed at Colemans Farm, Porchfield, burying itself deeply into the ground on impact. The pilot Flt Lt C.E. Bowen baled out safely. The same team of aircraft enthusiasts carried out a much larger scale dig at this site during 1982, this time aided by a JCB digger. On this site however, the wartime recovery team had done a very efficient clearance job and very little was found of the aircraft on this occasion.

Warmwell-based 152 Sqdn lost two Spitfires, both Mk Is, Flt Sgt J. Christie was killed when K9882 crashed into the sea to the south-west of the Needles. Flt Lt E.C. Deansley was shot down at 16.40 hrs. The aircraft, K9982, fell into the sea south of the Needles whilst Deansley, having abandoned the aircraft in an injured state, was rescued from the sea.

The Luftwaffe lost three fighters and one bomber in this area. Bfl10-C4, serial no. 3U+AR, works no. WN3094 from 7/ZG26 became yet another aircraft to crash at Tapnell Farm near Freshwater, its crash site being so close (within approximately 100 yards) to that of Moeller-Friedrichs Bfl09 crash of 18 August that subsequent aviation recovery groups found that the wreckage from both machines had over-lapped. Its crew, consisting of Lt Konopka and Uffz Eiberg, were killed. Again this aircraft was subject to the attention of the air enthusiasts in 1982. When the digger removed the top soil, a trail of aluminium crystals led to the bulk of the recoverable items which amounted to a DB601 engine, an undercarriage leg and the remains of a parachute. The second DB601 was found buried a few feet away from the main crater. The aircraft wreckage had been badly burnt and most of the rest of the wreckage amounted to no more than crystallised aluminium.

An interesting story related to the researchers whilst they were digging suggests that the troops guarding the wreckage had a lucky escape; they apparently left the wreckage to get food from the NAAFI tea wagon. Whilst they were gone ordnance within the wreckage exploded; their tea break had almost certainly saved their lives.

Another Bfl10 from 1/ZG26 came to earth around 16.30hrs at Bleakdown near to the Chequers public house at Rookley. This aircraft, serial U8+HH, had been hit by anti-aircraft fire during its bomber escort mission to Southampton Docks. As it made its approach towards the Downs, the crew apparently scattered farmers attending a local sale with an inaccurate burst of machine gun fire. Following the aircraft's force-landing, its crew consisting of FWs Rohde and Feber were captured by troops who were billeted locally. The same troops also removed the time fuse that the crew had set in an attempt to destroy the aircraft. One or two small parts of this machine are part of a private collection of wartime aviation records and artefacts held on the Island. This was the crash that the wheel mentioned earlier as being dug up at Rookley was at first assumed to have come from.

The last of the fighter escort to be lost that day was Bf110, serial no. 5F+CM, work no. 2187, from unit 4/(F)14, which crashed into the sea at SaltMead ledge in Thorness Bay, near Cowes. A local boat put to sea to attempt a rescue but the aircraft had sunk without trace. The crew, Lt Pank and Uffz Schmidt, were both killed; one in the sunken aircraft and the other when his parachute failed to open.

The sole bomber loss was that of 2/KG55s Heinkel HE111H, G1+GK, which was reported as lost in the western Solent following combat with Hurricanes from 229 Sqdn. Its five crew members, comprising Obltn Schwartz (Graf Von Schwientz?), Uffzs Widmann and Schab, Gefrs Helfer and Wastian were posted as missing.

The afternoon of 28 September 1940 saw a dogfight develop off the south-east coast of the Island between Hurricanes of 213 and 238 Sqdns and Bf109s. Four Hurricanes were shot down, all crashing within a couple of miles of each other; the Germans on this occasion suffered no losses. Hurricane V6776 from 238 Sqdn at Middle Wallop, was initially hit in combat over Fareham and went down in flames to crash into a small copse on the north side of Culver down. The aircraft made a shallow impression in the hard chalk and flint hillside, scattering wreckage over an area of about 300 square yards. Small fragments are still to be found by those with a keen eye as they travel the footpath towards the monument to the Earl of Yarborough.

The luckless pilot, Sgt Bann, who at twenty-six years of age was a veteran of the fighting in France, baled out of his stricken aircraft but was killed when his parachute failed to open. He plummeted to earth near Centurion's Copse on Brading marshes, approximately a mile from the crash site of his Hurricane.

238 Sqdn lost two Hurricanes. At 14.50 hrs, P3836 was shot down over the Solent in an engagement with the Bf109s. Its pilot, P/O D.S. Harrison was originally posted as missing. His remains were eventually washed ashore at Brighton on 9 October 1940. The second Hurricane, N2400, crashed into the sea at Forelands, off Bembridge, its pilot, Flt Sgt Little, was killed. Roughly one and a half miles to the south of this crash, Tangmere's 213 Sqdn pilot P/O James McGill Talman DFC was more fortunate when he was rescued from the sea after his machine L1770 crashed into Whitecliff bay. Twenty-two-year-old Talman from Dumbartonshire, a veteran of the fighting in France, had fallen victim to return fire from a Bf110 he was engaging over the Island. He baled out unhurt and was picked up by the Bembridge Lifeboat, which landed him at Ryde. The RNLI log for this event shows that this rescue was very swift. The Lifeboat was launched at 14.47hrs in choppy conditions to go to the aid of a 'British Aeroplane' two miles south of the lifeboat house and that one person was rescued; the lifeboat returning to its station at 16.00hrs.

Monday 30 September 1940, saw the loss of Junkers Ju88A-1, 4U+MH, from unit 1(F)/123, which crashed into the sea off Ventnor during a reconnaissance mission. The reason for the loss of Lt Frenzel's aircraft is unknown.

The next day saw another German loss when Messerschmitt Bf110D from 1/Zg26 was shot down into the sea to the west of the Island by RAF fighters, its crew of Lt Scharnhorst and an unnamed NCO perishing in the crash.

The early evening of 9 October saw the loss of Bristol Blenhiem IVF, N3530, from 235 Sqdn, which was attacked and shot down by enemy aircraft whilst on airfield protection patrol to the south of Portsmouth's Thorney Island airfield. The three crew, P/Os Kirkpatrick and Thomas and Sgt Keel, all lost their lives

Wednesday 15 October was an overcast day. Around mid morning Bf109Es of 3/JG2, on a freelance sortie looking for targets of opportunity, passed to the west of the Island en route for the Dorset coast.

On their return one of the German fighters was intercepted by a Hurricane from 145 Sqdn, which inflicted sufficient damage to the 109 to cause the pilot to force-land at Bowcombe Down near Newport. This aircraft, works number 1588, marked 'Yellow 8' and emblazoned with a cartoon drawing of Mickey Mouse wearing boxing gloves, was the regular mount of F/W Franz Jaenisch, who as the Mickey Mouse emblem indicated was a veteran of the Condor Legion and had seen action in the Spanish Civil War. However Jaenisch was busy that day celebrating his 100th mission and had let his 'personal' aircraft be flown by F/W Horst Hellriegel whose own aircraft had been declared unserviceable by his ground crew shortly before the mission was due to start.

Hellriegel emerged from the relatively intact fighter with only slight injuries and walked the mile or so to the nearest road where he gave himself up to the driver of a passing lorry.

Contemporary reports vary somewhat as to the details of the events following his surrender – Jock Leal and Adrian Searle in their books, relate that the pilot surren-dered to a coal lorry and was taken to the Waverely public house to await the arrival of the police and military; whilst the *Isle of Wight County Press* of 18 October 1940, carried a quite long and detailed report, by wartime standards, which differs in several respects.

The *Isle of Wight County Press* article names the driver of the empty cattle lorry as nineteen-year-old Harold Blow, who recalled that the pilot emerged from a hedge in front of his lorry and held his hand up to indicate surrender. Blow at first thought that the person was an allied pilot, but on closer inspection of his uniform and on hearing his broken accent realised that he was a German. After searching him for any weapons he put Hellriegel into his lorry and drove to the local village policeman's house.

On the way into town Hellriegel explained that had intended to walk into Newport as he knew the area well, his pre-war employment had been on liners which had docked at ports in the area.

The local policeman was out so Blow then drove to his own house at Gunville where he phoned the police, whilst his mother watched over the pilot. While they awaited the arrival of the police and army, Mrs Blow gave the downed pilot a meal of cold meat and Hellriegel, in return, offered her small daughter sweets and chocolate. Meanwhile, Hellriegel's aircraft, which was virtually intact on landing, had been ravaged by local souvenir hunters before the arrival of a military guard.

A Mr Farrington, who was employed locally in aircraft manufacture, gave an inter-esting personal account of this incident to me. In part of a long and interesting letter detailing several such incidents he wrote:

> *I was one of the young chaps that hurried on foot to the spot. The plane was facing east and I remember being struck by the bright coloured nose, the painted shield on the right hand side with the mouse with boxing gloves on, the long zip under the wing. The difference in the metal and riveting to the ones I was working on. Some one soon got to work with tin snips but failed to remove the mouse. Two young chaps walked home with the engine cover held over their heads and two more that lived near me had ammunition belts; the police later recovered these. For my part I had hoses and clips from the engine and some of the grey painted metal that had been removed plus one of the incendiary bombs from on the down which had failed to go off.*
>
> *I unscrewed the flat nose end under water in Plaice stream and removed the white powder and was suprised to see the date on the side was 1931 or 1932.*

He went on to say that he believed the aircraft was eventually put on display in Canada. A radio mast 'liberated' from this aircraft at the time of the crash was amongst several small components of this aircraft that were donated recently to the Kent Battle of Britain Museum.

15 October 1940 saw one other victim. An unidentified German bomber was reported shot down into the sea just off the Shingles bank in the Needles passage. Reports of this incident are very sketchy. A brief mention in *Fort Victoria; 1852 −1969* by Anthony Cantwell suggests that two of the crew baled out, but gives no indication of what happened to them, and that the pilot was killed in the crash and his body brought ashore at the fort. An entry in the form 540, for the Special Duties Flight based at Christchurch for that day, gives the following details:

> *Air raid siren sounded, Hurricane L1592 airborne at 12.20hrs. Encountered approx. 24 ME109s at 12000ft. one of which detached to attack. No combat. Returned to base 12.35hrs. Weather 9/10ths, cloud base 8000ft. Enemy engaged by Spitfires. One enemy aircraft seen to fall into sea. Thought to be Me110. One parachutist seen descending towards Lymington direction. Combat drifted eastward. 12.50 all clear sounded.*

Confirmation of a Me110 loss on this date has not as yet been discovered. However, as Ju88 L1+CK was lost around this area that day, this may well be a case of poor aircraft identification.

The Battle of Britain officially ended on 31 October 1940, the Island's involvement in it finished four days earlier. The 27th saw Ju88s escorted by Bf109s involved in an attack on Portsmouth. Hurricanes from Tangmere's 145 Sqdn engaged the attackers, losing three of their number in the battle. Flt Sgt D.K. Haire waded ashore unhurt after his aircraft, V6888, went into the sea 100 yards off shore at Forelands near Bembridge. Although the wreckage sank quickly, soldiers stationed locally managed to recover its radio equipment. The remainder of this aircraft was subsequently salvaged and became a ground instructional airframe (for trade skills training) and was re-serialed 2333M.

P/O F. Weber was picked up safely by a local launch after parachuting from his aircraft, V7592, before it plunged into the sea off Seaview. Approximately five miles to the east of the Forelands crash P3167 crashed into the sea close to the Nab Tower lighthouse. Its Belgian pilot P/O J.A. (Alexis) Jottard was killed. His best friend, P/O Jean Offenberg, with whom he had fought in Belgium at the start of the war, possibly witnessed this incident. Offenburg recorded the incident in one of the note books that he kept :

> *At about 17.00 hrs, in the same section [as Jottard] I climbed once more to 25,000ft. We had not been up 5 minutes before a formation of MEs dived on us out of the blue. We were over the south coast of the Isle of Wight.*
>
> *At the instant I half rolled to the left, I saw a Spitfire★ in a vertical dive with a long trail of smoke pouring from its tail.*

Offenburg and his wing man were attacked at this moment by three Messerschmitts, one of which was targeted by Offenburg, who poured tracer into it from around 300 yards, seeing large parts flying off the fuselage and smoke pouring from its right wing before he momentarily blacked out. When he regained his senses the sky was empty. He claimed the 109 as a 'probable'.

The sole German loss of the day was to be the last enemy aircraft to crash in the vicinity of the Isle of Wight during the Battle of Britain. This somewhat dubious honour went to a Bf109E from 3/JG2, which is reported to have fallen victim to anti-aircraft fire, but may in fact have been from the incident described above, and crashed into the sea off the Island, killing its pilot, Gruppe Adjutant Obltn Wolf.

Endnote

★ Offenburg refers in his text to seeing a Spitfire going down, however, of the five Spitfires recorded as destroyed on 27 October 1940, none were from squadrons operating in that area. It is likely therefore that what he recalled in the heat of battle as a Spitfire, was actually a Hurricane – and was more than likely that of his friend Jottard.

Chapter Four

The Next Phase

November 1940 to December 1941

Although the Battle of Britain had ended, the German bombing raids continued and aircraft losses in this area were to remain high throughout November 1940.

The first batch of November's losses occurred on the afternoon of the 6th when EGR210 sent approximately seventy Bf110s, with a fighter escort of Bf109s to bomb Southampton. The raid was met by Hurricanes of 145 Sqdn from Tangmere, and in the ensuing combats two Hurricanes fell to earth within two miles of each other with contrasting consequences. Flt Sgt K. Haire, flying V6627, was attacked to the east of Newport by a Bf109. His aircraft was seen to pass over the middle of the Island towards the Arreton Valley. The aircraft was by now ablaze and heading for houses in the village of Arreton. Flt Sgt Haire stayed with the aircraft in an attempt to steer it clear of the village and baled out only when it seemed that he had achieved his goal. The village was saved from damage, Haire's aircraft crashed into a field at Perreton farm near to Hasely Manor. The fate of the pilot was a different matter. In his brave attempt to save civilian lives, he had left it too late to bale out successfully, his partially opened parachute crashing him into the ground only yards from the burning wreckage of his Hurricane. His injuries were so severe that he was to die before medical help could get to him. Only eleven days earlier, on 27 October, his luck had been considerably better when he had waded ashore unhurt from his crashed Hurricane at Forelands.

Within minutes a Bf109 that had been chased from the area of Haire's crash by another Hurricane was seen to fall into the sea at Monks Bay near Ventnor. This was Bf109E Black 1+ from 5/JG2 and was almost certainly the aircraft that shot down Haire. Its pilot F/W H. Klopp did not live to claim his victory.

Almost simultaneously, Havenstreet's Air Raid Precautions post was recording the fall of the second Hurricane. This was R4177, which slammed into the north side of the downs above Duxmore farm near Ashey. Its pilot, Flt Sgt J. Weber, was unhurt. By a strange coincidence another pilot from 145 Sqdn, P/O F. Weber, had crashed into the sea off Seaview on the same day and within three miles of Haire's crash at Forelands. Twice in eleven days Haire had crashed almost at the same time and within a few miles of another pilot called Weber!

7 November 1940 saw another attack launched against Southampton. Around 100 Bf110s, with their customary escort of Bf109s, crossed the Island during the afternoon en-route to their target and were again intercepted by the Hurricanes of 145 Sqdn, whose vigorous defence saw one Bf109E downed at a cost of five Hurricanes. The German pilot from 3/JG2 was killed when his fighter crashed into the sea to the south-east of St Catherine's Point.

145 Sqdn lost P/O A.N.C. 'Nigel' Wier DFC, who was killed when his aircraft, P2720, plunged into the sea at Woody Bay near Ventnor. Despite the fact, that Wier's aircraft apparently crashed only around 100 yds offshore, his remains were never found. Wier was a published poet, Faber & Co. of London subsequently published a selection of his works in 1941 under the title *Verses of a Fighter Pilot*. While approximately a mile to the north-west Flg-Off D.B. Sykes was to escape with relatively minor injuries when P2924 crash-landed at Old Park St Lawrence. Five and a half miles to the north-east, Flt Lt Bungay was injured when he force landed V6889 into the sea close to the beach at Littlestairs Point, Shanklin.

Mk I Hurricane R2683 was damaged by a Bf109, and came down at an unspecified location on the Island. This machine was recovered fairly intact and converted to a Mk II (serial BV163). 145 Sqdn's final loss of the day was P2770★, which crashed into a disused chalk pit at Ashey Down, close to the site of the ill-fated Bindorffer's Bf110 crash. P/O J. Ashton escaped unhurt from this incident.

The next day saw the loss of an unknown British fighter aircraft when it ditched into the sea off Forelands near Bembridge. No more aircraft were to come down in this area until nearly the end of the month.

The evening of 24 November saw Portsmouth's Anti-Aircraft guns in action against German raiders returning from the Bristol area. Heinkel He 111H-4, work number 3092, serial G1+KN from II/KG55 was hit as it passed over the Solent and crashed into the sea off St Catherine's Point at 19.40hrs. Its crew, comprising Obfw Werner Muller, Lt Gerhard Heiland, Sfw Heinriech Heidt, Sdf Emil Weihmuller and F/W Heinreich Gaick were posted as missing.

The early afternoon of the 28 November saw Major Helmut Wick leading his fighter unit, Stab/JG2, on a 'Frei Jagd' (free hunt) mission in the Isle of Wight area, looking for contact with any British aircraft. Wick was an accomplished pilot with fifty-four victories to his credit and had become 'Geschwaderkommodore' of JG2 on 20 October and had recently been awarded the Eichenlaub (Oak leaves) to accompany his Ritterkreuz medal. Wick was at the time considered to be the most famous 'Experte' of the Luftwaffe.

Around 15.10hrs, the unit reported being in combat with British fighters and claimed three shot down for no loss, one of which was claimed by Wick. It would seem probable that their adversaries had been from 213 Sqdn, who reported a Hurricane lost into the sea off St Catherine's Point, and from 602 Sqdn, who reported a pilot killed under unknown circumstances. Following this combat, Wick led the 'Richtofen' unit back to base to re-arm and refuel their aircraft. They were soon back over the Island looking for further victims. Wick's unit was flying at high level to give it the maximum advantage in an attack. A formation of Spitfires was sighted below and Wick formed his squadron into loose pairs and dived to the attack. Wick's chosen target filled his gunsight and one burst of 20mm cannon and 7.9mm machine gun fire impacted into the Spitfire of 609 Sqdn's P/O Baillon sending the aircraft and its pilot to a watery grave south-west of the Needles. Helmut Wick's fifty-sixth victim was to be his last. His speed had carried him past the Spitfires and one of them chased after him and opened fire. Rudi Pflanz, Wick's wingman, was not close enough to prevent the attack and saw his leader's aircraft hit and watched as the cockpit canopy spun away from the 109. Pflanz pursued his leader's attacker out to sea and shot the Spitfire down.

Other German pilots in the Geschwader reported seeing Wick fall clear of his doomed aircraft and successfully open his parachute. In the ensuing battle, they had no further chance to watch out for their leader and Wick was never found. This engagement has long been a subject of conjecture by air historians over the sequence of events and who shot down whom, more than one pilot seeking the accolade of downing Germany's top ace. Bearing in mind the frantic nature of dogfighting at close quarters this is perhaps not surprising.

The generally accepted view of the battle is that 609 Sqdn sustained the first attack: P/O Baillon was suprised and shot down by Wick; Flt Lt John Dundas, in Mk I Spitfire X4586, chased and shot down Wick's Bf109E, work number 5344, before himself falling victim to the guns of Wick's wingman Pflanz. Another Spitfire unit, 152 Sqdn had arrived shortly after the battle commenced, and they were to lose two aircraft. Mk I Spitfire P9427 was shot down into the sea to the south-west of the Island killing Flt Sgt Klein, the second pilot P/O Watson suffering an identical fate. Sixty years to the day later, on 28 November 2000, a memorial to Flt Lt Dundas was dedicated and unveiled on the cliffs above Freshwater Bay.

602 Sqdn's loss from the earlier combat may well have been P/O M. Lyall, who was killed after baling out too low when his Mk I Spitfire N3242 crashed at Rill Farm near Whitely bank. The aircraft suffered Category 2 damaged and was recovered and converted to a Mk 5 and reissued to 603 Sqdn. It was lost in the sea approximately a year later, on the 9 December 1941. Also lost into the sea off St Catherine's Point was Hurricane V6691, its pilot, Flt Sgt Barrow, was reported as missing.

The next incident was to occur on 19 December when a Bristol Beaufort Mk I, serial L9823 from 217 Squadron, ran out of fuel whilst returning from a mission to Bordeaux and ditched into the sea three miles south of the Needles.

Three days later the same fate was to befall a Bristol Blenheim 1F night fighter, L6686 from 23 Sqdn, based at Ford in West Sussex, whilst on patrol to the south of the Island on 22 December. The pilot, Flt Sgt Loveridge, gave the order to abandon the aircraft and his two-crew members baled out just off the coast near Ventnor. Loveridge followed shortly afterwards and drifted down to a safe landing near Ventnor. His crew, Flt Sgts Newman and Southall, were not so lucky; they had both landed in the sea and were unfortunately drowned. Meanwhile the pilotless Blenheim flew on and eventually crashed onto Brading Down.

The New Year of 1941 started with night raids on the usual south coast targets as well as overflights by units attacking targets further north. No losses were recorded in the first two months of the year.

Memorial to John Dundas, unveiled at Freshwater Bay on 28 November 2000. (A.T. Gilliam)

Bristol Beaufort Mk I. (Air Britain)

The first loss of the year was on 13 March and was recorded somewhat vaguely in the 'Form 540' operations log of Christchurch's Special duties flight. It recorded: '23.00 hrs. Enemy a/c on fire at 8,000 ft. heading south over Christchurch. Crashed into sea between Needles and Mudeford beach.'

The *Isle of Wight County Press* carried the following brief report which would seem to relate to this incident: 'At about 23.00hrs on Thursday night an enemy bomber making its way home was seen to burst into flames, break in two and crash into the sea south of the Needles. Mr J. Cotton, a fisherman of Freshwater Bay, put out in his boat but could find no trace of the machine or its occupants.'

Nine days later, on 22 March, another Blenheim came down onto the Island due to mechanical problems. This time the aircraft and its crew fared much better. V5396 from 59 Sqdn, based at Portsmouth's Thorney Island, landed at Brook. The crew was unhurt and the aircraft, having suffered only minor damage, was dismantled and removed by an RAF maintenance crew.

A brief report in the book *Isle of Wight at War* mentions the loss in the early hours of Saturday 5 April, of an unidentified German bomber. The bomber jettisoned its entire bomb load into the sea off Freshwater in an attempt to escape from an attacking fighter. The attempt was in vain, the German bomber swiftly followed its bomb load into the sea.

This aircraft may have been Junkers Ju88A-5, work no. 4224, V4+AR of III/KG 1. This bomber was tasked with attacking Avonmouth and was intercepted by an airborne radar equipped Beaufighter of 604 Sqdn. The Junkers disintegrated in the attack and pieces of wreckage hit the attacking Beaufighter. It crashed into the sea south of the Needles at 00.50hrs on 4 April, its crew, Lt Ernst Menge and Uffzs Wilhelm Hahn, Robert Konig and Wilhelm Schrieber, were listed as missing.

Just before midnight on the 10 April P/O G.C. Budd, patrolling in a 609 Sqdn Bristol Beaufighter from Middle Wallop, intercepted and attacked a Heinkel HE111, 6N+HL, from 3/KG100 pathfinder unit based at Vannes in Brittany. The Heinkel was returning from leading a raid on the Midlands. The aircraft caught fire and subsequently broke up at around 1,500ft. The bulk of the wreckage crashed at the Hermitage, Whitwell, at 23.45hrs close to the spot where Avro Anson K6246 had crashed in January 1940 whilst other parts came down up to a mile away. Out of the crew of five, three had baled out but only one managed to successfully open his parachute, the last two crew members' bodies were found inside the wreckage. F/W O. Kuntze (pilot), Lt H. Tretow, Obltn H. Klingenfuss and Gefr H. Kiersh, were all killed. The surviving crewman, F/W H. Hank, landed safely and despite a concentrated search effort eluded capture until the following afternoon when he was arrested in Ventnor.

Supermarine Spitfire II. Serial P7666. This is an example of a presentation Spitfire. This particular aircraft carries the name Observer Corps. It was on the strength of 54 Sqdn until shot down off Harwich on 20 April 1941. (Authors Collection)

15 April 1941, saw the loss of P/O A.R. Ross from 610 Sqdn at Westhampnett. His Mk II Spitfire P7684 was listed as 'failed to return from operations' following its crash into the sea at Spithead off Ryde whilst intercepting a Dornier Do215.

616 Sqdn suffered the loss into the sea of Spitfire Mk IIA, P7812, when on 21 April 1941 it was abandoned off the Island following combat with a Bf109.

Six days later, a Ju88A-1, work no. 0294, F6+AM from unit 4(F)/122 was attacked and shot down into the Solent by a Beaufighter flown by P/O D.O. Hobbs of 219 Sqdn. It crashed at around 22.30 hrs, taking its crew of Lt Berger, F/Ws Reicherzer and Klier, and Gfr Paulke to a watery grave. One of the propellers from this aircraft is on display at the Southampton Hall of Aviation following its recovery from the sea at East Dean Sands, off Southsea.

On 28 April, H. Flight of No.1 AACU based at RAF Christchurch lost Fairey Battle K9320 when it crashed into the sea at 15.45hrs some 300yds offshore at Hengistbury Head following an engine failure, its pilot, P/O A.C. James, was killed.

A further seven days later, on 5 May, Wellington T2908 from the Fighter Experimental Establishment based at Middle Wallop ditched just yards offshore at Boscombe. This accident was caused by a maintenance error at Farnborough. The fuel tank ground servicing cocks were inadvertently left in the closed position, this gave the pilot a false indication that there was an adequate fuel supply in the tanks when they were in fact empty causing the engines to stop through fuel starvation. Fortunately, there were no serious injuries to the crew who all waded safely ashore. The only crew details traced are those of the pilot who was Flt Lt Hayley-Bell.

In the early hours of 8 May, Alfred Lord Tennyson's former home Farringford House at Freshwater, had a lucky escape. Around 01.30 hrs. a Heinkel He111, serial 1G+CC from 2KG/27, returning from a night raid on Liverpool crashed near to the house. The aircraft created a large crater and was totally destroyed. Of its crew of four only Obfw H. Laube was to survive, injured, to become a POW The remaining members of the crew; Uffzs K. Dillinger, A. Habeareiter and W. Range, were all killed. The Heinkel had been intercepted by a Beaufighter from 600 Sqdn, its pilot Flg-Off Woodward, had chased the He111 for forty miles across Hampshire before getting into an attacking position. A burst of fire from the Beaufighter stopped the Heinkel's port engine and brought return fire, which punctured the Beaufighter's fuel tanks. The He111 dived and was briefly lost to view, when contact was regained its port engine was seen to be ablaze. A second attack caused the flames to spread and the Heinkel dived into the ground.

A shallow depression still marked the crash site in 1982 when a team of aircraft recovery enthusiasts undertook a 'dig' at the site. The field itself was scattered with small remnants and a large amount of wreckage, including an undercarriage unit complete with its Dunlop tyre as well as both engines, was recovered from the excavation. The recovery of the engines somewhat suprised the team as wartime records clearly showed that they had been recovered and delivered to a salvage depot in Weybridge!

During my research for this book I received a letter from a Mr John McGannicle relating to this incident in which he states:

I was a New Zealand Naval pilot under training in 1941 in the Fleet Air Arm. On a short leave from HMS Vincent *at Gosport, I hired a bike at Ryde with the intention of cycling around the Island.*

Having difficulty finding overnight accommodation I spent a most uncomfortable night on the 8th May 1941 under a haystack in the Farringford area in the west [of the Island]. There was a lot of aerial activity and anti-aircraft – I presumed a raid on Southampton. It was also very cold.

Next morning I headed towards Alum Bay and noticed a number of military personnel on the right, not far off the road, and on stopping I realised that it was the site of a crashed plane which turned out to be a Heinkel 111.

Being in uniform, I was able to wander around and I established there were three aircrew still in the wreckage. It appears the Heinkel went straight in, as there was a very deep crater with not a lot of wreckage strewn around. No sign of the engines etc.

Mr McGannicle concludes that he wonders why he did not take a photo at the time. But he did recover a few small bits and pieces from the crash, which he still has – including some damaged bullets, a parachute harness buckle and an instrument knob inscribed 'Geschwindigkeitsmessung' (speed measuring).

After the war, Mr McGannicle returned safely to New Zealand where he still resides.

Three days later, at 01.30hrs on the 11th, the night raiders suffered another loss. Ju88 B3+LH from 1/KG54 was shot down over the Solent by anti-aircraft fire and plunged into the sea close to Egypt Point at Cowes. Only one body was recovered, that of Gefr P. Adomat. He was buried in Parkhurst Military cemetery until the end of the war, when his remains were exhumed and re-interred at Cannock Chase (German Military cemetery). His fellow crewmen, Uffz L. Muth, Gefr Tischendorf and F/W K. Stiebitz, were posted as missing.

Freshwater saw the destruction of another Ju88 on 29 May 1941, when 7T+JH from 3/KG606 was intercepted whilst returning from a night raid in the north by a patrolling Bristol Beaufighter. The Ju88 was successfully attacked and crashed at 23.55hrs onto Wellow Down killing its four-man crew of F/W F. Christiansen, Uffzs H. Kubler and A. Wagemayer and Obfw R. Manigel.

The official enemy aircraft crash report for this incident states that at that time the cause of the crash was unknown and that the aircraft struck the cliff top in the dark and the central portion of the fuselage caught fire. No bullet strikes were detected on any part of the wreckage. Due to the extensive damage caused by the fire, the only markings that were discernible were the letters '2g' in red atop the fuselage just ahead of the fin. Of the five machine guns and one cannon that this type carried only two mg-15 machine guns were recovered from the wreckage

The *Isle of Wight County Press* for 31 May briefly reported the incident in the usual vague way of the war years: 'During Thursday night a Junkers 88 crashed on the top of Downs near a south-coast holiday resort.' The report goes on to state that the aircraft's petrol tanks exploded and the wreckage was completely destroyed by the fire.

There was a heavy ground haze that night and the reflection of the burning plane in this haze had the curious effect of appearing that a huge fire was burning in the sky.

Crash site of Ju88 7T+JH, Wellow Down, (29 May 1941). The stones at the bottom of this pit are still blackened by oil and fire from the inferno following the crash. (A.T. Gilliam)

The site of this crash is still clearly discernible. The aircraft crashed into a disused pit alongside the footpath that skirts the woods on the top of Wellow Down. Sixty years later, the loose scree in the pit is still blackened and oily from the fire.

June 1941 was to prove a tragic month for the allied airmen in this area with no less than three aircraft destroyed, all with fatal results.

The first incident was a mid-air collision on 11 June between two Fleet Air Arm aircraft on a daytime exercise over Spithead. The aircraft involved were a Grumman Martlett (Wildcat) AL254 from 881 Sqdn F.AA based at Gosport and piloted by Lt J.A. Rooper, and a Fairey Fulmar, N1924 from 800 FAA also from Gosport and crewed by Sub-Lts T.P. O'Donovan and L.H. Morris. The collision took place over the airfield at Lee on Solent, both aircraft crashing into the sea at Spithead. The subsequent rescue attempt failed to locate the remains of the three aircrew.

On the 23rd Polish pilot P/O S. Szmejl, from 32 Sqdn based at Ibsley in the New Forest, was killed when he flew his Hurricane Z3396 into the cliffs at a fog-bound Freshwater Bay. Stanislaw Szmejl was an experienced pilot. He had trained at the Cadet Aviation School in Deblin (Poland). In September 1939, as a pilot of 114 Fighter Escadrille, he had helped to defend Warsaw and following the fall of Poland saw action in France.

7 July saw three Heinkel He111s, from the German pathfinder unit KG100 based at Vannes, shot down into the sea to the south-west and west of the Needles. The aircraft were returning from a raid on the Bristol area. The aircraft and crew details were: 1G+AF, crew Uffzs K. Lammert, H. Erdwey, Gefrs. J. Pitzke, R. Schmidt; 6N+GK, crew Obltn G.H. Franke, Fws Richard Hartel, Paul Stien, Adam Wetzell, Sdfhr A. Kapfhammer; 1G+AP, crew Uffzs A. Assmuth, H. Teschner, Gefrs M. Petry, W. Gilkert and A. Blecha. Out of these fourteen aircrew only Obltn G.H. Franke was to survive to become a POW, Kapfhammer, Wetzell, Stein and Hartel were buried at 11.00hrs on 11 July at Christchurch cemetery in Dorset.

At around 06.00hrs on 24 July Junkers Ju88, 4D+CH from 1/KG30, force landed at Yaverland. It was returning from a raid on Birkenhead and had drifted off course, possibly because the RAF had successfully jammed the 'Knickebein' and 'X-Gerät' radio beams that the Germans used for navigation and as a bombing aid. The aircraft had apparently orbited around the Thorney Island/Isle of Wight area for up to two hours before it finally circled low over the Sandown area two or three times prior to its landing in a corn field. A local sixteen-year-old youth, Mr Geoffrey Janes, was shooting rabbits in the immediate area and quickly made his way to the crash site meeting up there with another local rabbit hunter, Mr Stanley Woodnut. Janes told an *Isle of Wight County Press* reporter:

> *I saw the plane circling round preparing to land. As it came down one of the crew threw back the cockpit cover, got out and sat astride the fuselage, as it landed he jumped off. The other three then got out of the plane and came towards me. I threatened them with my gun, and two of the Nazis, who had automatics, started waving them about. They were all four very young. I tried to take the automatics off them but they would not give them up. I said, 'You had better come to Bembridge Fort with me.' Just as we moved off Woodnut came up.*

Stanley Woodnut reported that one of the Germans spoke good English and asked if they were in England. The crew told Janes and Woodnut to get well away from the wrecked bomber because they had set a demolition charge to destroy it. The German crew and their civilian captors ran some 200yds and had taken cover before the aircraft caught fire and exploded. The machine was completely destroyed from just behind the nose section back to the tail.

The German pilot told Woodnut that his aircraft had been hit during a raid in the north of England and that the fuselage was damaged. They had lost their way and did not know where they were landing. The aircraft had ploughed through the standing crops on landing and further damage was caused to the crop by the ensuing fire.

The crew of Lt W. Deiderich (pilot), Uffz H. Wiedeman and Gefrs H. Riecke and W. Wildemann were all uninjured and became POWs. The official crash report states that the aircraft had taken off in good weather from Lanveoc-Poulmic at 23.15hrs for an objective on the west coast of Britain but on the outbound flight the weather had deteriorated. Shortly afterwards the radio failed and the crew having become completely lost, jettisoned their bomb load into the sea at around 02.00 hrs. The crew confused the Bristol Channel with the English Channel and on reaching the Island thought they must be over France (except for one member of the crew who thought they were over Lands End). The Military report states that the crew's morale was fair and that they were not as truculent as other aircrew they had encountered and also gave the impression that they were not very experienced.

It is interesting to note that another aircraft from the same Geschwader landed at Broadfields Down aerodrome near Wrington in Somerset after also thinking they were over France.

On 1 August 1941 a Fleet Air Arm Blackburn Roc, Serial L3126, from No.2 Anti Aircraft Co-operation Unit based at Gosport side-slipped into the sea off Eastney whilst making a low turn. Its RAF pilot, Sgt T. Jankowski, was rescued safely from the sea. The two-seat, turret-armed Roc was designed as a Fleet Air Arm equivalent to the Boulton Paul Defiant and suffered a broadly similar fate. The relatively low top speed and lack of forward firing armament saw the majority of Rocs relegated to training roles and target towing duties.

A Westland Lysander, T1439, from the Special Duties Flight at RAF Christchurch suffered engine failure and ditched twelve miles south of Steamer Point at 12.25hrs on 20 September. The aircraft had been on radar trials to measure propeller modulation for the anti-aircraft gun laying GL3 radar system. This require the aircraft to fly very slowly at low engine revs which in turn caused the spark plugs to foul. The pilot, Flt Lt A.M. Dunlop, was rescued but his observer, Sgt A.G. Russel, was listed as missing presumed drowned.

The next few months of 1941 were incident free, nothing of note happening until November when a Taylocraft (Auster) serial HH983, light communications and army co-operation aircraft, crashed onto Brading Down injuring its two occupants.

One of the last incidents of the year was to be yet another tragic accident. In the early evening of 22 November, two patrolling Hurricanes from Tangmere's No.1 Sqdn roared in from the sea over the Ryde area. Passing low over the area that is now

Taylorcraft Auster: Communications and Army Co-Operations aircraft. (A.T. Gilliam)

Binstead housing estate, the aircraft suddenly pulled up to avoid a row of tall trees. The rear aircraft came up under the tail of the leader and its propeller sliced away the tailplane. One of the Hurricanes, BD940, crashed a few hundred yards away into the grounds of St Wilfreds, a large house at the end of Playstreet Lane. Its pilot, Flt Sgt L.J. Travis, had not been able to exit from the aircraft and died in the crash. The other pilot fared better. Flt Sgt D.F. Perrin, although injured, managed to bale out before his aircraft, Z3899, crashed a little farther on into a field alongside Dame Anthony's Common on the outskirts of Ryde.

The final crash of the year in this area was that of an as yet unidentified Vickers Wellington bomber that was reported to have been destroyed in an explosion just off the coast at Forelands near Bembridge late in the evening of 6 December.

Endnote

* Previous works have listed this machine as P2683; however, P2683 is recorded as being lost in France in May 1940. This error may well have arisen through the loss on the same day of R2683

Chapter Five

The Final War Years

January 1942 to October 1945

The New Year of 1942 saw a change in the way in which the aerial war was waged. The large scale German raids were giving way to hit and run attacks carried out by smaller numbers of fast fighter bombers using their small but deadly bomb load, coupled with indiscriminate strafing with cannon and machine gun fire. Being unpredictable and of short duration, these type of attacks were harder to detect or to defend against. This fact coupled with the increasing number of allied aircraft using the airspace around the Island as the war progressed towards the ultimate invasion of Europe and beyond was to result in a decreasing number of German aircraft coming down whilst the number of Allied crashes remained fairly high.

The first loss of the year occurred on 4 January when Blackburn Roc L3143 ditched into the sea off Hayling Island. The aircraft crashed when the engine failed whilst climbing away from a dummy dive bombing attack and was declared Cat.E following the crash and SOC eight days later on the 12th. The pilot Sgt B. Travell was uninjured. Like the previous Roc crash some five months earlier, this aircraft was also from No.2 Anti Aircraft Co-operation Unit based at Gosport.

Bomber Command suffered two losses in the early months of the year. The first occurred when on the night of 14/15 February, a Handley-Page Hampden 1, serial AE397 from 49 Sqdn ditched into the sea off the Island. The bomber, call sign EA-G, had taken off from RAF Scampton on a bombing mission to Mannheim, and on its return ran out of fuel forcing the pilot to ditch the stricken machine. The crew consisting of P/O Allesbrook and Sgts Stanbridle, Wilkinson and Woolgar, were reportedly uninjured.

The second, very similar, incident took place exactly two months later when a 106 Sqdn Avro Manchester, L7317 call sign ZN-? ran out of fuel while returning from an operation over Dortmund. The Manchester had taken off from its base at RAF Conningsby at 22.40hrs on 14 April and radio failure during its mission caused the bomber to be hopelessly off track on its return flight. The crew, comprising P/O J.A. Worswick, Flt Sgt Spiby and Sgts Jones, O'Hare, Hutchieson, Goodings and Cartwright, were attempting an emergency landing at the Fleet Air Arm base, HMS *Daedalus*, at Lee-on-Solent, when their fuel finally ran out and they ditched into the sea one mile short of the airfield threshold. The crew survived their ditching without serious injury.

Between these two incidents, the Fleet Air Arm also suffered two accidents. The first of these occurred on 9 March when Fairey Swordfish II, serial DK687, from 825 Sqdn was engaged in a local flying exercise. The aircraft was flying low over the Solent and bounced off the sea, subsequently stalling back into the water from around 30ft killing its unfortunate crew of Sqdn Ldrs D.W. Adams and C. Richardson. The second incident also involved a Fairey Swordfish II, serial DK691, also from 825 Sqdn, which became lost in conditions of low visibility and its Pilot decided on a precautionary descent before falling victim to the local high ground. The ensuing force-landing saw the machine overturn in marshy ground near Godshill. Its crew, comprising Sqdn Ldrs N.S. Hutchings and R.H. Teuton, emerged unhurt from their experience.

The date given in FAA records for this incident is 17 March 1942; this is at variance with the addendum to H.J.T. Leal's book, which records the incident as happening on 20 April. FAA records show the machine as one of a production run of 100, contract built by Blackburn Aircraft Ltd and delivered from the manufacturers to Worthy Down on 17 January 1942, joining 825 Sqdn at an unspecified date in January 1942. DK691 was shown as returned to Royal Navy Aircraft Repair Yard (RNARY) Fleetlands at Gosport on 21 April for repair following this incident so this may well account for the April date previously attributed for this crash.

On 22 April 1942, a photo-reconnaissance Spitfire made a 'wheels up' landing at Borthwood Copse. The aircraft, X4492, a Mk PR VI, coded D-P, came to rest on the south side of the copse near to Sandown Airport. The eyewitness who related this to me remembers that the machine bore a light colour scheme (typical of recon-naissance aircraft) and was substantially intact. The 140 Sqdn Spitfire operating out of RAF Benson had been on an operational sortie when it suffered an internal Glycol (coolant) leak in the engine. Its pilot, P/O F.J. Blackwood, successfully force-landed the machine which suffered Cat.B damage. The aircraft was recovered and records show it as serviceable again by 29 June 1942. In fact this aircraft went on to have a fairly long career; built at Eastleigh as a Mk F1a, it first flew on 14 July 1940 and subsequently passed through several modifications before eventually ending up in Canada as a Mk FV1.

An interesting addendum to the records for this aircraft show that on 9 July 1945, this aircraft was flown from RCAF station Rivers (Manitoba) on operation Eclipse. Piloted by Flt Lt Tom Percival at 35,000ft over Lake Winnipeg, the aircraft attained a (then) record height for photographing a solar eclipse. The photographs later appeared in *Life* magazine.

Around a fortnight later mechanical failure again played a part in the loss of an aircraft. Around midnight on 2 May 1942, Middle Wallop-based Bristol Beaufighter X7693 from 604 Sqdn was patrolling off the south-west coast of the Island when its starboard propeller became loose and flew off. P/O W. Howard-Williams and his crewman baled out of their stricken machine before it plunged into the sea near the Needles and were picked up by a rescue launch.

The night of 4/5 May saw heavy bombing in and around Cowes with scattered attacks at other locations around the Island. At Ventnor a Dornier Do217 was caught and attacked by fighters and jettisoned its bomb load on and around the sea front in an attempt to escape. Its actions were in vain; the Do217 joined several of its country's aircraft that night when it was seen to crash into the sea south of Dunnose Point. The *Isle of Wight County Press* for 30 May 1942, carried a brief report that the bodies of three German airmen had been washed ashore at Atherfield, Bonchurch and Sandown. One was a youth of about eighteen-years and wearing an Iron Cross, they had been in the sea for between one to three weeks so it is possible that one or all of these unfortunate crewmen came from aircraft lost on that night.

The end of the month saw another German fighter down onto the Island when at 15.20hrs on 27 May; a Bf109F-4 from 10/JG2 crashed near Sandown. The fighter/bomber had been one of a group of three on an anti-shipping patrol over the Solent and had attacked a destroyer, its bomb missing its target by mere yards, when it was itself attacked by three Spitfire VBs from 41 Sqdn. P/O J.J. Allen was the first Spitfire pilot to engage and crippled the 109 with five bursts of fire from his machine guns. With smoke pouring from its engine, the enemy aircraft turned back towards the Island. Allen realised that the German pilot intended to force-land his stricken machine and ordered his wingmen not to press home the attack. For some reason one of his wingmen, Flt Lt Wainwright, did not heed this order and poured more devastating fire into the aircraft.

The pilot Lt Fröschl was forced to bale out but his parachute failed to open and he was killed. Reports as to where he fell differ somewhat; two sources (IWCP & HJT Leal) state that he fell into a copse near to Yaverland church whilst Adrian Searles's book records the location as 'near the sea wall at Yaverland'. The aircraft came to earth at Yaverland Manor Farm burying itself deeply into the ground in what had once been a tulip field. This aircraft carried the identification markings Blue 4+, (works no. 7626) and had a squadron emblem consisting of a Grey ship held firmly in the mouth of a red coloured fox. A dig carried out in recent times at the site by aircraft recovery enthusiasts found that the wartime recovery team had been very efficient on this occasion, the remaining items at the site barely filling a carrier bag!

10 June 1942 saw two Spitfires from 41 Sqdn based at Merston in West Sussex crash onto the Island. The first was Mk V Spitfire AR377 that crash-landed at Rowborough Farm, Brading. Its pilot, Flt Sgt W.A. Wright, was removed, injured, from the damaged aircraft by locally based soldiers. The aircraft was recorded as suffering Cat.E damage and was struck-off-charge on 12 June. It was subsequently repaired and spent time with various squadrons before finally stalling into the sea off Littlehampton on 22 July 1944.

The second Spitfire, also a Mk V, was AD504 which crashed near a property called Belvedere at St Lawrence, near Ventnor. Flt Lt D.W. Wainwright was removed severely injured from the wreckage and taken to the nearby Royal National Hospital at St Lawrence where he unfortunately died from his injuries. This aircraft was an example of a 'Presentation machine' that had been bought for the nation by monies collected through local fund raising (Spitfire funds). This particular machine had been paid for by the Nottinghamshire District Miners' fund and carried the name 'Notts Miner'. Records show AD504 was SOC on 12 June.

Later that month another Mk V Spitfire crash-landed. This was EN965 from Tangmere-based 118 Sqdn which force-landed at Atherfield, its pilot, Flt Sgt D.C. Eva escaping uninjured from the incident. H.J.T. Leal and other sources list this incident as happening on the 17th, although the aircraft's record card shows it as a Flying accident causing Category A damage and occurring on the 26th. This machine was recovered and repaired, serving in several squadrons before finally being converted in February 1944 into a trainer.

Tragedy struck again towards the end of July when on the 28th two Gloster Gladiators from 2 Anti Aircraft co-operation Unit from Gosport, collided whilst on a training exercise off the coast at Culver, near Sandown. The aircraft were K7985 and L8030 and the pilots, Flt Sgt Chapman and P/O R.A. Flood, were both killed.

19 August 1942 saw sporadic German raids on troop ships and naval vessels returning to the Solent area from the ill-fated raid by Canadian Commandos on Dieppe. One German bomber crashed onto the Island. Junkers Ju88 M2+FH, Works no. 140178, from 3/KG106 based at Chateaudun was hit in the rudder by anti aircraft fire as it made a north to south attack towards Portsmouth Harbour, the Ju88 jettisoned its bombs and headed over the Island.

The anti-aircraft fire over the Island was intense and the bomber was hit again, this time in the port engine which stopped dead. The aircraft was now down to about 250metres in fog and rain and with very little control left, it passed over the centre of the Island and crashed at around 19.00hrs into Wroxall copse, ploughing through the trees and coming out the other side. Soldiers were quickly on the scene and recovered the crew from the wreckage.

Uffz W. Hase died from his injuries, the remainder of the crew, Lt E. Kegenbien and Uffzs E. Ostereich and W. Arnold, were taken seriously injured to the Royal National Hospital at Ventnor where following treatment they passed through a series of military hospitals before finally becoming POWs.

Six days later, at around 05.30 hrs, two Ju88ds flew through early morning mist over the southern half of the Island. Mount Joy ROC look out post at Newport reported hearing the aircraft but could not get a visual confirmation of them due to the thick mist. The machines were heard to turn south-east whilst somewhere in the area of Godshill. The Sandown look-out post then reported hearing aircraft going back out to sea again. However, only one aircraft was to leave the area. Some $2\frac{1}{2}$ hours later, the wife of the farmer at Wroxall farm was mushrooming when she heard cries for help coming from a ditch. In the ditch, she found an injured German airman, Uffz Mobius, who, despite a broken leg and arm had crawled nearly a quarter of a mile to get help for his fellow crewmembers. At about the same time the farmer had discovered the wreckage of the Junkers Ju88d 4U+GH from reconnaissance unit 1(F)123 near to the summit of St Martins Down. Despite the valiant efforts of Mobius, his crewmen: Lt Beeg, Uffz Schwartz and Gefr Scherler had perished in the crash. The two aircraft had approached low through the mist and, as had been the case before in this area, one aircraft was fortunate enough to miss the high ground, the other had not been so lucky.

The early hours of the morning of 9 September 1942, saw a confrontation between Bristol Beaufighter V8265 and an unidentified Heinkel He111. The 141 Sqdn Beaufighter had taken off from Ford in Sussex at around 01.30hrs to patrol the Channel south of the Island. At 02.00hrs they were vectored onto a possible hostile. At 02.03hrs the aircraft's radio operator, Flt Sgt Edmund 'Terry' Walsh, reported a contact at three miles distance. W/O Russell 'Lofty' Hamer piloted his aircraft towards the radar blip and visually identified it as a He111. Hamer opened fire and saw several strikes on the target, including hits on the starboard engine, which burst into flames. The Heinkel put up a determined defence gaining hits on the Beaufighter's cockpit area and starboard engine. Part of the German bombers wing sheared off and flew backwards striking Hamer's aircraft and making it swing violently. The He111 succumbed to Hamer's continuing attack and rolled onto its back before plunging into the sea at approximately 02.15hrs some twenty to twenty five miles south-west of the Needles.

Hamer had been badly injured by the return fire from the Heinkel. He had lost the use of his right leg and very little feeling in his left arm. The Beaufighter was also badly damaged. With flames streaming from the starboard engine, Hamer turned the aircraft northwards and headed for the safety of Beaulieu airfield. He feathered the propeller on the burning engine, which successfully put out the fire. However, as he

Handley-Page Halifax BIII. (Air Britain)

approached the northern coast of the Island the engine once again burst into flames. Hamer ordered Walsh to bale out of the stricken machine, holding the aircraft steady long enough for Walsh to exit safely from about 1,000ft. Shortly after Walsh jumped, the port engine failed and Hamer radioed to say that he had no chance of escaping himself. The Beaufighter crashed at Boldre, near to Lymington. Hamer died instantly in the wreckage. Walsh's parachute deposited him into a barbed wire emplacement on the coast near Newtown. After extricating himself from the wire he made his way to the nearest farm where having first convinced the local farmer that he was not an enemy airman he was taken to the Headquarters of the local anti-aircraft battery.

The afternoon of 1 November was a typical winter's day, fog and sea mist clung to the southern side of the Island. At 14.45hrs, two Mk VI Spitfires from Westhampnet's 616 Sqdn were returning from patrol, flying low and in close formation they entered into a bank of fog. Within that fogbank was the high ground of Stenbury Down at Wroxall. The two Spitfires ploughed into the summit within 50yds of each other. Flt Sgt S. Smith, in BR186, was killed instantly, his wingman Flt Sgt K. Rodger, in BR174, was seriously injured. Both aircraft were recorded as sustaining Category E damage.

7 November 1942 claimed another victim. Fairey Albecore I, Bf634, from 823 Sqdn, Fleet Air Arm based at Lee on Solent, had taken off from Tangmere on a vectoring exercise with RAF aircraft when it suffered engine failure south of the Island and ditched into the Channel. Of its crew of two, Sqdn Ldr A.W. Stewart was rescued safely, tragically his crewman, Midshipman R. Redfern did not survive.

Five days before Christmas, six members of the Royal Canadian Air Force lost their lives in yet another tragic accident. Their aircraft, a Handley Page Halifax, serial W7768 from 405 Sqdn, which at that time was on secondment to Coastal Command, had taken off at around 06.30hrs from Beaulieu airfield in the New Forest for an anti-shipping mission. Shortly after take off the aircraft was heard passing over the western end of the Island. The large bomber apparently suffered serious engine failure and before the crew could do anything to save themselves, Halifax G – *George* plunged vertically into the ground at Eades farm, Newbridge and exploded in a ball of fire. Two bodies and most of the bomb load were thrown clear. Rescuers who arrived at the scene could do nothing for the crew, who comprised of, Flg-Off F. Stollery and Flt Sgts L. Snarr (pilot), H. Croft, N. van Brunt, N. Fugere and G. Wagner.

The first incident of 1943 emphasised the difficulty of instant aircraft recognition in wartime when P-51 Mustang AG389 from Dunsfold's 400 Sqdn, was shot down on 20 January in another 'friendly fire' incident. The fighter was attacked and shot down into the sea to the south of St Catherine's Point by two Hawker Typhoons, killing its Royal Canadian Air Force pilot, Flg-Off J.B. Ferris.

Two days later, on 22 January, a Bomber Command aircraft crash-landed in a field at Elanor's Grove, near Quarr Abbey, close to the main Ryde to Newport road. The crew of four sergents was taken to Ryde County Hospital where they were treated for their injuries, although only Sgt S.W. Wood needed hospitalisation. The other crewmen, Sgts H. Pilkington, G.W. Sivell and H.S. Fidge, escaping relatively unscathed. The aircraft, a Lockheed Ventura II, serial AE876 and call sign SB-N,

North American P-51 Mustang. (Air Britain)

from 464 Sqdn, had taken off from Feltwell aerodrome at 12.20hrs to attack Maupertius Airfield near Cherbourg and was hit by flak near the target area, returning from the bombing raid on just its port engine it had apparently been trying to reach the airfield at Lee-on-Solent but was forced to come down several miles short.

On 7 February the 'magnet' that appeared to reside at Wroxall Farm attracted its latest victim when Dornier Do217e U5+GP from unit 6/KG2 crashed into St Martin's Down to become the fourth aircraft to crash within three quarters of a mile of this farm. The Dornier had been on a mine laying operation around St Catherine's Point. The aircraft turned inland and flew low over Rew Down, where it disgorged its last sea mine. The mine devastated Appuldurcombe house to the west of Wroxall, leaving the once impressive country-seat of the Worsley family a roofless ruin. The house was never repaired and is now owned and maintained in its derelict state by English Heritage.

The Do217 flew over Wroxall farm barely above roof top height and crashed into the down at around 22.10hrs. The farmer and his wife were once again the first on the scene of the crash and searched the wreckage for survivors. There were none; the crew of four F/W Salz, Uffz Jendis, Gefr's Gröschel and Teubner had all perished in the crash.

Hawker Typhoon 1B. (Air Britain)

An official report document (form EA/30) dated February 1943 outlines the crash and gives detailed information on the aircraft sub type and several modifications found on it. It states: Do.217-E2. U5+GP.

This aircraft crashed at Wroxall farm near Ventnor on 7 February 1943. It struck the top of a hill at a fine angle and broke up, the wreckage being scattered down the succeeding hillside. Both engines rolled to the floor of the valley and were much damaged. The fuselage had broken into three sections and the tailplane and fins had been torn off. On the fin was painted U5+GP 5315 and a plate in the starboard wing tip identified the machine as a Do 217 E-2. However both the battery cases bore the marking Do 217 K and work no. 4433-CF+PF.

The report surmised that the batteries had been transferred from another aircraft but did suggest that the crashed machine could have been a K type variant due to the armament and other modifications discovered on it.

Among the modifications discovered on this aircraft were a previously unseen propeller de-icing arrangement, large high frequency cables leading from two automatic switches marked 'Heizung R' and 'Unformer R' on the radio switch-panel out to the wing tips and a switch and wiring arrangement for the explosive jettisoning of the wing bomb carriers which had not been found on any previous examples of the Do 217. The camouflage scheme of this machine was dark green upper surfaces with spray painted black lower surfaces and fuselage sides, the propeller spinners being dark green with a yellow tip.

A month later, on 7 March, Fairey Swordfish II, HS313, from the Fleet Air Arm's 836 Sqdn, took off from Thorney Island on a minelaying sortie. Whilst off Culver Cliffs at Sandown, the pilot was momentarily blinded by a coastal searchlight and flew into the sea killing his two crewmen, Sqdn Ldr W.B. Muir and Leading Airman E.R. George; the pilot Sqdn Ldr R.A. Singleton was rescued safely following a five-hour ordeal in the water.

5 May saw a Spitfire make a satisfactory emergency landing near to Hale Common, between Arreton and Apse Heath. The aircraft was apparently forced down through engine trouble and the pilot was unhurt. The private notes of H.J.T Leal, to which I was kindly allowed access, records this aircraft as being serial DP845. If this is correct then this machine was the prototype Griffon-engined Spitfire, which was operated on test flying out of Boscombe Down. Assuming this to be the case then the aircraft could not have suffered any significant damage in the emergency landing as no flying accidents or damage categories are listed for that date on the record card for this aircraft. This particular Spitfire went on to be yet another prototype when it was later converted to become the first F Mk XII.

25 May saw another aircraft forced down by mechanical problems when Tangmere based Hawker Typhoon 1B serial DN303 from 486 Sqdn force landed on Brading Marshes. The pilot, Flt Sgt D. Bennett, was unhurt in the landing and was able to extricate himself from the aircraft and walk to the nearby St Helen's Railway Station to report the incident by phone to his base.

Two aircraft were lost on 16 August. The first incident was the loss of Boulton Paul Defiant DR896 from 1622 flight, anti-aircraft co-operation unit, based at Gosport. The Defiant was a two-seater fighter aircraft, equipped with a power operated four-gun turret behind the pilot but with no fixed forward firing armament, that had failed to live up to expectations. Following several terrible maulings at the hands of German fighters it had at first been relegated to night fighting usage at which it fared much better and subsequently to training and general duties such as target towing for gunnery practise. The aircraft was on such a mission when it crashed into the sea off the gunnery ranges at Eastney killing its two-man crew that comprised of Flt Sgt Shaver and one other crewman.

The second incident involved some very accurate shooting by the heavy anti-aircraft guns at Whippingham and/or Nettlestone. During the early evening three Bf109Gs flew over Portsmouth to photograph the results of the previous evenings bombing raids. As the aircraft turned back over the Island, they were flying at around 38,000ft in a beautifully clear blue sky.

The 3.7in radar predicted guns opened fire at the three fighters some seven miles above them. One shell was seen to detonate directly below the leading aircraft. This incident was watched by a large number of people who had been alerted to the overhead activity by the sound of the guns, and much cheering was apparently heard when the Messerschmitt was hit. The Bf109 was totally destroyed in mid air with wreckage strewn over a considerable area around the Newchurch locale. The body of the luckless pilot, Lt H. Jaschinski from unit 4(F) 123, was found at Kern Plantation near to Knighton still strapped into his seat whilst the engine apparently plummeted to an undignified end in the manure pit at Hill Farm near to the present-day site of Alverstone Garden Village. The two wings floated down to earth reasonably intact and were found, inspected and relieved of small items for 'souvenirs' by locals (although reports as to the exact location vary, one source stating that they were found in two adjacent fields close to Ashey down, another correspondent told me that he found one wing in Bloodstone Copse).

Many rumours abounded after this shoot down that the Bf109 had actually fallen foul of a high-flying fighter. A Beaufighter or Mosquito have been suggested, and that when found, the wings were riddled with 20mm cannon shell holes. Although one recent letter in the IWC Press from the brother of one of the locals who found the wings stated that this was definitely not the case. This was however, believed to be the only 'G' variant 109 to crash onto British soil. An altimeter, believed to be from this machine is in a private collection of artefacts held by a local enthusiast.

Another Messerschmitt Bf109G/4 was lost on the 14 September when it was attacked by two Hawker Typhoons and shot down into the sea off St Catherine's Point. The aircraft was from unit A(F)123 and bore the unit marking 312+, its pilot Obltn F. Wittmer was posted as missing.

At 17.50hrs on 4 October 1943, 434 Sqdn Halifax II, serial DK250 call sign IP-W, took off from RAF Tholthorpe tasked with a bombing raid to Frankfurt. This

De Havilland Mosquito TT35. (Air Britain)

Lockheed P-38 Lightning. (Air Britain)

machine never returned to base. It crashed into the English Channel with the loss of all seven crewmen on board. Four bodies were later washed ashore onto local beaches from Ventnor to Hayling Island, the remaining three crewmen being commemorated on the Runnymede Memorial for crew who have no known resting place.

Flt Sgt L.S. Clarke (RAFVR) was injured when his Tangmere-based 197 Sqdn Hawker Typhoon JP844 crash-landed near Garstons Farm to the south-west of Newport on 5 November.

Previous books on Island air crashes relate that on 27 November, a Lockheed P-38 Lightning became the first American-operated aircraft to crash onto the Island. They report that this incident happened just as dusk was falling when a formation of P-38s was returning from a sortie; as they flew in over Compton Bay in bad visibility one aircraft had insufficient height to clear Compton Down. The aircraft was destroyed by fire following the impact and the pilot perished. I can find no reference to any lost P-38s in this area for that date. However, an eyewitness to the aftermath of a similar accident accompanied me to Wellow Down, (about one mile inland from Compton) and pointed out the original impact site and subsequent wreckage trail over the side of the Down.

A brief inspection of the area at the bottom of the steep hill side provided one small piece of wreckage, still bearing its US Airforce green paint. The eyewitness,

Mr G. Foskett, told me how, as a youth, he had attended the crash site and collected a few 'souvenirs' but he was sure that the date I was quoting had to be wrong. He had not lived in the area until at least a year later and that when he visited the site the foliage was in full growth, so November could not be correct. Also the aircraft had to be outbound, for the wreckage trail ran roughly north to south, the tail of the aircraft remaining on the crown of the hill, whilst the two Allison engines lay in the field at the very bottom of the Down. Further research uncovered the loss of two P-38s from the 393 Fighter squadron of the 9th Airforce's 367 Fighter Group in the area of the Isle of Wight for 25 June 1944. Lt Liotta, flying a P-38 J-15-LO, serial 43-28702, was on his first mission when he slammed into the very top of Wellow down in bad weather. The unfortunate pilot was killed instantly. The second P-38's loss was also believed to be in this area but other than the pilot's name, Capt Pierce, no further details are known.

Definitely lost on 27 November 1943, was Halifax II JD164, call sign AL-K. This 428 Sqdn machine had taken off from RAF Leeming at 16.50hrs on a mission to Stuttgart and was hit by flak at 20.30hrs when some ten minutes short of the target causing damage to one of the port engines.

The pilot managed to get the aeroplane back to the south coast but whilst attempting an emergency landing at Thorney Island they came down short of the airfield and ditched into the sea. No injuries were reported amongst the crew that comprised Flt Sgt P.A. Charlebois (RCAF), Flg-Off J.W. Cameron, and Sgts J.D. Moss, J.H. Senecal, M.R. Neville, D.P. Lambert and J.M. Leith.

Around lunchtime on 2 December, Mustang FD508 from Middle Wallop-based 63 Sqdn, attempted an emergency landing at Somerton airfield. The airfield was being extended at the time of this incident and the Mustang collided with earth moving machinery being used by the building contractors. The aircraft turned over onto its back in the crash and was badly damaged. The injured pilot, Flg-Off J.S.B. Wright, was removed from the wreckage by men from the contractor's workforce.

Somerton airfield was involved again at the end of December, when on the 31st an American Lockheed P-38, low on fuel, attempted an emergency landing at the 'works' airfield. The P-38, one of three aircraft, circled the field before attempting to land. The pilot decided to overshoot on his first attempt and as he climbed away from the field his engines cut and he crashed into Ruffin's copse to the west of the airfield. The pilot, Capt. Richard C. Garrett, escaped without any serious injuries and managed to free himself from the wreckage just before it burst into flames. Once again the contractors men rushed to assist the pilot and saw him taken safely away from the crash site. The aircraft were from the 20th Fighter group based at Kingscliffe in Northants and were returning from a bomber escort mission over the Bordeaux area. This 1,300-mile round trip from their Northants base was the longest mission yet attempted by the group. The distance stretched the aircraft to the limits of their operational range causing seventeen out of thirty-one aircraft to divert to other bases due to low fuel; including one successful landing at Somerton.

One local report states that aircraft from 20th TFW over flew Somerton at low altitude the next day and dropped packs of 200 cigarettes as a thank you gesture for the help given to the downed pilot.

Capt. Richard C. Garrett, 20th Tactical Fighter Wing, escaped uninjured when his P-38 Lightning crashed at Gurnard, 31 December 1943. (20th TFW)

Capt. Garrett (nick-named Steamboat) went on to complete his tour of duty with the 20th Fighter Group on 1 August 1944, having amassed 303.25 combat hours and having been credited with 1 damaged Bf110. He was decorated with the Air medal with three clusters and the DFC with one cluster.

An entry in the 20th Fighter Group's unit history outlines the mission:

MISSION NUMBER 3. 31 December 1943. While 2 combat wings of 3rd Division Forts attacked important ball bearing and industrial targets in the Paris area this morning, 6 combat wings of 1st & 3rd Division Forts and 120 B-24s of the 2nd Division, on one of the longest 8th A.F missions to date, hammered at German airfield and control stations in the Bordeaux area and at La Rochelle.

On the longest fighter escort mission ever attempted,[to date. sic] 20th, 55th and 345th Groups were assigned the role of 'target umbrella fighters 'for the heavies bombing in the Bordeaux area. Led by Lt Col. Jenkins 35 P-38s took off from Kingscliffe at 0949hrs and met the bombers over the water just west of Bordeaux. They covered the target area for 20 minutes and set course for home at 12.35hrs.

The long haul left a number of the boys very short of gas as they came home. 4 landed at Exeter, 7 at Ford in southern England, 3 at Herrington and 2 on the Isle of Wight. Lt Garrett really sweated out the ride across the channel and actually used his last ounce of gas over the south coast of the Isle of Wight, and crashed in a cabbage patch on the Island. He's ok though and should be home tomorrow. Steamboat reports that if it hadn't been for the splendid moral support and encouragement of Lts Bond and Hart, he might well have abandoned his plane in France.

A second American aircraft was lost on 31 December 1943. This was a B-17G, serial 42-31064 nicknamed 'Hey Lou', from the 401 bombardment group based at

Deenethorpe. The bomber, which was on only its sixth mission, was damaged by flak during a raid on Kiel and was seen to crash into the sea off the Island. Only one body, that of co-pilot two, Lt J.S. Dockendorf, was recovered. The remaining nine crew members were listed as missing in action.

The P-38 crash at Somerton was the second American accident in two days. On the previous day a Boeing B-17 bomber, serial 42-31149 from the 388th Heavy Bombardment Group stationed at Knettishall in Suffolk, whilst returning from a bombing raid on the I.G./Farbenindustrie Chemical Works at Ludwigshaven, had radioed ahead that it was in desperate need of an emergency landing site.

The Island Observer Corps had advised that no such site was available on the Island and the B-17 was advised to make for Beaulieu airfield in the New Forest. Beaulieu initiated its emergency landing procedures and indicated its position by switching on two searchlights, their vertical beam piercing through the low overcast in an attempt to guide the stricken aircraft towards the now illuminated runway.

The observer corps post at Niton reported hearing the B-17 passing overhead en route to its New Forest haven but could not see it due to the low cloud base. Then as the aircraft passed over the Island it began to turn and head back along its inward route.

Niton ROC post reported the B-17 passing overhead once more and then filed its report that the bomber had crashed into the sea some three miles off the coast. Of the crew of ten, only four Staff Sergeants, J.E. Mont (ball turret gunner), J. Payne, (right waist gunner), W.L. Steele (left waist gunner) and F.C. Zagrovich (tail gunner) survived to tell the tale of the B-17's last mission.

Forty aircraft from the 388th plus a Pathfinder element had set off on the mission, leaving Knettishall between 08.17 and 08.51hrs that morning. Six aircraft aborted the mission before reaching the French coast, the rest reaching the target and bombing blind through full cloud cover. A short time after 'Bombs away' Lt P.J. Commella in aircraft No.149, experienced trouble with no.3 propeller which set up a lot of vibration and caused the engine to catch fire. Commella put the aircraft into a dive to attempt to extinguish the blaze but in doing so the prop tore from its mountings and crashed into the nose section of the B-17.

As they struggled home, they were attacked by German fighters who scored hits on the no.2 engine, causing that to be feathered. By now, their altitude was down to 600ft. As they limped over the French coast on the two remaining engines their troubles increased when they were hit by anti-aircraft fire.

The pilot, Lt P.J. Commella, decided that due to the condition of his machine and the prevailing visibility a force-landing in the sea would be safer than an emergency landing at an airfield. Whether that decision, which took not only his life but those of Lts G.M. Claypool (co-pilot), W.K. Aunspaugh (navigator), C.C. Belfy (bombardier) plus Sgts P.R. Sacco (gunner) and F.C. Pilato (radio operator), was the right one is impossible to gauge.

The new year of 1944 was three months old before the next incident occurred. In poor visibility on 13 March an Armstrong-Whitworth Albemarle, Serial V1711 from 295 Sqdn at Hurn, flew into the high ground of St Catherine's Down. Flt Sgt Knowles was injured, the rest of the crew consisting of the pilot Flt Lt Kingdon and Flg Sgts

Muddeman, Bishop and Hulme escaped unscathed.

On 18 April a crash occurred just outside the area covered by this book, but the Island had a significant involvement before the shoot down and the event was sufficiently unusual to warrant its inclusion. At around 07.15hrs on this bright and clear morning radar stations in the area picked up a single hostile trace on a north westerly heading some miles to the south of Sandown. The Royal Observer Corps report shows the aircraft flying at just cruising speed as it passed over the coast at Culver at an altitude of around 4,000ft. Just inland from its crossing point it turned west and headed towards the centre of the Island until it reached Brighstone Down, where it turned north. As it did so it was reported to have fired a single red flare.

As the aircraft reached the Porchfield area it turned onto an easterly heading firing another flare as it manoeuvred. By this time the aircraft had attracted the attention of local light anti-aircraft batteries and considerable amounts of tracer rounds were fired at it. The German machine made no armed response and carried on its easterly course until it reached Ryde where it fired yet another flare before turning south towards Brading and Sandown where another flare was fired. It then turned onto a westerly heading towards Brighstone Down again where it fired its last flare as it turned towards the north.

The ROC report states that on its first circuit the aircraft was at around 1,000ft dropping at times on its second circuit to 500ft.

As the aircraft approached the northern coast of the island it was intercepted by two Typhoons from 266 Sqdn based at the relief landing ground of Needs Ore Point on the New Forest shoreline. As the Typhoons pressed home their attack with 20mm cannons the German aircraft made no attempt to return fire on them nor apparently did it take any evasive action. The German machine finally succumbed to the attack as it crossed the Hampshire coast and crashed into marshy ground close to Exbury house near the mouth of the Beaulieu River.

The machine was a Junkers Ju188E-1 Z6+EX, works no. 260523 from 2/KG66. When recovery teams arrived at the crash site the mystery deepened a little further. The crew had all perished in the crash but instead of the expected five bodies in the wreckage they found seven. In addition to the regular crew of Uffzs Johan Crispin, Johan Krauss, Robert Schultes, Eitel Wysotski and Gfr Hans Ehrhart were the remains of two ground crew – Gefrs Leonard Schwingenstein and Edgar Vester.

The official combat report of the incident varies in some details to that of the ROC's report. It states:

> *Aircraft shot down at 7.30 a.m. at Exbury House near Beaulieu. The aircraft was engaged by AA fire over the Isle of Wight at 9,000ft. The aircraft went into a shallow dive later being engaged by Typhoons. The A/C suffered 20mm. damage and crashed into water logged ground breaking up badly on impact.*

No mention is made in this report of the Junker's erratic flight path or its constant firing of flares. It does however confirm the number of crew on board at seven and not twelve as original ROC reports had claimed.

Martin B-26 Marauder seen bombing-up at a New Forest Airfield. (By courtesy of the Portsmouth Evening News)

Quite what the aircraft's intentions had been or why it carried two additional personnel in what would have been already cramped cockpit space has never been discovered. Several theories have been put forward ranging from the aircraft being lost, the crew were attempting to flee from the Luftwaffe and surrender or that the aircraft was from a special unit and was tasked with dropping agents or saboteurs into England. It is unlikely that the true facts will ever be known.

The next allied loss occurred when 329 Sqdn lost a Mk IX Spitfire, MK373, on 26 April. The fighter crashing into the sea off St Catherine's Point.

During the morning of 12 May a formation of B-26 Martin Marauders from the 387 Bomb Group of the United States Ninth Air Force, based at Stoney Cross airfield in the New Forest, crossed the Island on a southerly course. Local reports state that when the formation was some ten miles south of St Catherine's Point one of its number turned back and jettisoned its bomb load into the sea. The B-26 recrossed the Island coast and crashed between Billingham and Kingston to the north of Chale Green.

However, information provided to me by the 556 Sqdn of 387 bomb group gives a slightly different version of the incident.

The records of the 556 reveal that the aircraft was a B-26B variant and carried the serial 42-96910. The flights' mission was to attack coastal gun positions at Barfleur-La Parnelle on the Cherbourg peninsula. During the mission, the B-26 became unstable and the co-pilot, Lt Hanna, and the bombardier, Lt H.J. Hallnon, baled out whilst the aircraft was over the Cherbourg peninsula.

The pilot, Lt E.G. Bond, brought the aircraft back across the Channel before baling out 'over Southern England' along with the four remaining crewmembers. The report concludes that the aircraft crashed onto the Isle of Wight and that the five crewmen returned to their base the next day.

A recent conversation with an eyewitness of this incident revealed further details of this crash. The aircraft was seen approaching from the south, over the English Channel, and once over the coast of the Island began circling whilst the crew members baled out. The doomed aircraft then went into a near vertical dive before impacting into an earth bank on the south side of Bucks Farm. The eyewitness, a Mr Draper, was about half a mile from the impact site and remembers seeing one of the machine's engines cartwheeling across the field. The aircraft caught fire and was totally destroyed. The young Mr Draper was advised by the pilot not to approach too close to the scene as ammunition was 'firing' off and there was at least one bomb left aboard the aircraft. Despite this danger, members of a Royal Signals Regiment unit that were stationed nearby bravely searched the crash site for survivors.

That evening the five American crew members, dressed in borrowed Signals Regiment uniforms, were taken to the Crown public house in Shorwell by their army hosts, where they chatted and drank with the locals.

The pilot of a flak-damaged Typhoon 1B, MN761, from 193 Sqdn was forced to abandon his aircraft fifteen miles Southeast of the Island on the 5 June. Just twenty days later, 193 Sqdn lost another Typhoon 1B in the area. This was the consecutively numbered MN760, which was presumed to have ditched on the 25th in low cloud following a fighter sweep one mile south of the Needles. In between these two incidents, on the 23rd, yet another Typhoon 1B was lost. This was EK218, from 198 Sqdn, which ditched south of the Island following engine failure.

7 June 1944 saw a spate of accidents, the first of which was the force-landing near to Ashey Racecourse of an A-20 Havoc. The aircraft was undamaged in the landing and was flown out from the site following repairs.

Later that same day Typhoon 1B, serial MN735, from 182 Sqdn based at the advanced landing ground at Needs Oar Point in the New Forest, crashed at Ashen Grove Farm near Calbourne whilst returning from a mission over France. Its pilot Flg-Off W.J. McBean (RAAF) was unhurt.

Also on 7 June a Mk IX Spitfire NH183 from 421 Sqdn was reported as having left its formation off St Catherine's Point and was officially listed as 'failed to return' from operations.

Four days later South African pilot Flt Lt R.A. Cummings was not so lucky as the Typhoon pilot had been. He was killed instantly when his Mk IX Spitfire, MJ219 from Tangmere's 229 Sqdn, clipped the chimney of a farmhouse at North Grounds Farm, Chale Green, the aircraft sliced through the tops of some nearby trees before ploughing into a field. The aircraft had roared in through low cloud and mist from the direction of Chale and crashed at around 14.45hrs

Less than a week later, on 16 June, another Spitfire pilot tragically lost his life in an accident within around ten miles of the previous incident. MK V Spitfire AB208, from 130 Sqdn, bearing the name *VC Lancastria Avenger 1* was involved in a mid air collision with Spitfire W3128 six miles south of St Catherine's Point. W3128 was able to return to its base. AB208 was not so fortunate, plunging into the sea, its pilot, Flt Sgt G.M. Ferguson (RAFVR), was posted as missing. The missing Spitfire had up until this point had a fairly long and much modified history. Its first flight was recorded as having taken place on 20 December 1941, since when it had modifications to its fuel system, rudder, elevators and bomb racks. It had suffered a category A flying accident on 21 July 1942 and had only been with 130 Sqdn since 22 May that year, having previously passed through various Maintenance units.

Brading was the scene of the next incident when a burning aircraft was seen in difficulties over the area. The pilot was seen to bale out from the stricken machine and float to earth on the nearby marshes where he was found to have suffered only minor injuries. The *Isle of Wight County Press* of 29 July 1944 carried the following report:

> *Much excitement was caused in the Brading district on Saturday evening [22/7/44] when a plane that was in difficulties over the east Wight, from which the pilot had baled out, fell in the garden of the vicarage and burst into flames. Part of a burning wing landed on the vicarage roof, but this was promptly removed by civil defence workers and others.*

The NFS (National Fire Service) from Ryde and Sandown were quickly on the scene and eventually succeeded in putting out the flames but not before the aircraft was practically burnt out. The plane when it crashed demolished about 30ft of a high wall separating the Vicarage garden from a playing field and uprooted a fruit tree. A hole was torn in the Vicarage roof and part of a chimneystack broken off. Fortunately the Vicarage was uninhabited at the time, the Venerable C.W. Hampton-Weeks (Archdeacon of the Island) being on the mainland and the staff being out. The only casualty was the pilot of the plane.

He came down by parachute in the marshes and sustained injury to an ankle. Spectators say they saw one of the engines of the plane on fire before the pilot baled out.' In fact, unbeknown to the eyewitnesses or the *Isle of Wight County Press*, a second aircraft had been involved in this incident. The two aircraft, American P-38-Js from the 9th Airforce's 370 Fighter group, forming part of the second element of a large formation had taken off on a combat mission from their airbase at Andover.

At 18.44hrs, they were over the sea approximately five miles west of Selsey at around 2,500ft and climbing towards heavy overcast. As they climbed into the overcast, 1st Lt Leonard Murphy, flying serial No. 42-67943, suddenly noticed the number two aircraft in the formation, serial 42-67456, flown by 2nd Lt Marvin Burr, slip erratically to the right. Burr's aircraft narrowly missed Murphy's and disappeared from view. Seconds later it came sliding back to the left. Murphy's right-hand propeller sliced into the cockpit canopy of Burr's machine, which then disappeared down into the cloud base. Lt Murphy also started to descend through the overcast, to try to make landfall. Murphy's propeller had sheared off and his engine was smoking badly. Conscious of his full fuel load he decided to bale out from the stricken aircraft.

Murphy drifted down on his parachute and landed alongside a gun-site about a mile from the outskirts of Brading, spraining his ankle in the landing. He was taken to see the wreckage of his P-38 and the damage to the vicarage before being transferred to Somerton Aerodrome at Cowes where he was collected and flown back to his base.

Meanwhile 2nd Lt Shaffer, flying No.4 position in the formation, had heard Murphy's frantic radio message that he had suffered a collision with Burr and tried unsuccessfully to raise either of them on his radio. Shaffer and another pilot descended through the overcast to search for their friends. All they found was an oil slick and floating debris in the sea some six miles east of the Island. Lt Burr and his aircraft were never found. The accident enquiry board laid the blame for the collision squarely on the shoulders of Lt Burr, and commented that Murphy had shown good judgement in abandoning his damaged machine.

At 02.10hrs on the morning of 28 August 1944, a Short Stirling, serial EF311, from 196 Sqdn based at Keevil, force-landed in the sea near to the Nab Tower off Bembridge. The Royal Canadian Air Force pilot, Flg-Off D.R. Campbell was returning from a mission over southern France dropping supplies to the French Resistance fighters when the Stirling suffered a port inner engine failure. He feathered the propeller successfully only to see the engine catch fire and continue to run on, the engine eventually oversped, causing its propeller to disengage from its drive shaft and fly off, damaging and stopping the port outer engine as it spun away from the aircraft. With marginal power and asymmetric thrust from the remaining two engines plus considerable drag from the damaged port outer cowling, Campbell decided to ditch in the sea rather than risk a night landing.

Flg-Off Campbell had brought the stricken bomber across the channel in total darkness, flying on instruments alone. Around ten miles from Selsey with the aircraft down to 500ft they put out an SOS and braced themselves for ditching. Campbell stated in a recent interview for the *Chichester Observer* that he could not see the water until they struck it. The bomber remained afloat and he exited from the escape hatch and swam to the wing where he found the wireless operator.

The rest of the crew was still inside the fuselage; they had been taught that when an aircraft ditched it would skip over the surface like a stone skimmed across a pond and were still sat tight awaiting further impacts. It wasn't until the air gunner declared that as the water was already up to his waist and he was getting out that the remainder of the crew crawled out of the fuselage and safely made their way to the rubber dinghy.

The crew floated aimlessly around for a while some seven miles off the coast before they managed to attract the attention of two local fishermen, the Lawrence brothers, who at first were reluctant to pick up the airmen in case they might be Germans who if armed may have forced them to sail to the Continent. Having convinced the fishermen with details of Aston Villa football team that they were indeed friendly forces they were picked up. Unfortunately the fishing boat soon ran out of fuel so a makeshift sail had to be rigged to sail the boat away from a danger that the lone airmen had not been expecting. The shoreline that they had seen and were hoping to reach under their own steam was mined! Campbell and his crew, comprising of Flg-Offs A.L. Capes, B. Leadley, Flt Sgts Dodds, F.J. Gladwin and S. McQuillan, were eventually brought safely to dry land at Selsey with only minor injuries and exposure. With the exception of Flt Sgt Dodds (RAFVR) the entire crew of this aircraft were from the Royal Canadian Air Force.

In August 1992, several members of the RAF Brize Norton Sub Aqua club accompanied by professional diver Martin Woodward from Bembridge attempted a dive on the remains of EF311. Working at a depth of around fifteen metres in conditions of poor visibility the team did quite a remarkable job of surveying the remains.

The wreck lies in an area of strong currents and considerable 'propwash' from passing ships had degraded the exposed parts of the aircraft's fuselage and tail surfaces. The divers discovered that with the exception of the upper fuselage sections the aircraft was substantially intact at and below seabed level. The wings had lost most of their upper skinning but the tanks and lower structure had stood up quite well, some of the fuel tanks still sporting their thick rubber 'self sealing' covering. One engine was detached from the rest of the wreckage and all of the engines had corroded badly. The team considered that if the removal of tons of this shingle and silt could be dealt with then the bulk of the framework lying buried beneath the shingle could quite probably be recovered.

14 September 1944 saw a minor accident at Somerton airfield involving a Tiger Moth from 41 Sqdn, based at Lympne in Kent. Whilst attempting a take off in extremely windy conditions the aircraft was flipped onto its back and wrecked. Its two-man crew scrambled from the wreckage with minor injuries. No confirmation of this incident have as yet been found; however Tiger Moth II, serial N9204, from 667 Sqdn is recorded as having crashed at Somerton some months earlier on 25 January 1944, in broadly similar circumstances.

The crash record states:

> *Blown round by gust on take off, Hit hedge and tipped up; Somerton, Isle of Wight. 25.1.44. This particular machine had started its days with 224 Sqdn then passed through Nos. 13 & 19 Elementary Flight Training Schools [EFTS] and No.1 AACU before going on to 639 Sqdn before finally ending up at 667 Sqdn; no mention being made of 41 Sqdn.*

So whether two separate Tiger Moth crashes occurred in 1944 at Somerton or just one crash with wildly conflicting details is hard to be certain.

The last recorded crash of 1944 involved Spitfire MK323, a Merlin 66 engined Mk IX from 84 Group Service Unit (GSU). The nine-month-old aircraft was reported to have suffered a flying accident on 11 November and crashed at Ryde sustaining Cat.E damage. The record source lists the cause of the incident as 'abandonment following fuel shortage in bad weather' but shows no specific location for this incident. A personal recollection of one of the many people who contributed information for this book related to a force-landed Spitfire at Cothey-Bottom (near to the present site of the Tesco supermarket) during the latter part of the war. It is possible that this may have been MK323.

The New Year was barely five weeks old when the weather was to play a major part in the next incident. On 6 February 1945 the American 339th Fighter Group were returning to their base at Fowlmere from an escort mission over Eastern Germany in 10/10ths cloud cover right down to 700ft with visibility down to less than 700yds. Two P-51D-10s Mustang fighters were lost over the Island because of the appalling conditions. 2nd Lt Gerald W. Palmer was killed when his aircraft, serial 44-14383 and named *Umbriago*, crashed onto the beach at Puckpool at 2.35 that afternoon.

Capt. Robert W. Bloxham's fighter, serial 44-13379 and named *Miss Idaho*, was not found until a week later. It too was on the sands off Puckpool, however it was empty. Capt. Bloxham was never found.

The *Isle of Wight County Press* carried two short reports relating to this incident. The first, from the paper of 10 February 1945 reported 'A torpedo bomber type of aircraft which was flying low and apparently in trouble over Seaview, crashed on the sands off Puckpool killing the American pilot. The plane believed to be an Avenger, caught fire and exploded.' The following week's paper stated 'ANOTHER AIRCRAFT FOUND OFF PUCKPOOL. About 600yds from where a Mustang aircraft crashed on the sands off Puckpool last week another aircraft was discovered at low tide on Tuesday. There was no occupant of the machine, which by its rusted

Capt. Robert W. Bloxham. Two American fighter pilots from Fowlmere based 339 fighter Group, killed in action when their Mustang aircraft were lost in poor visibility in the Puckpool area of Ryde on 6 February 1945. (Via J. Harris)

2nd Lt Gerald W. Palmer. (Via J. Harris)

state suggests that it had been in the water for some days.' The initial report of an
Avenger crashing is almost certainly a mis-identification of the first Mustang, the
second week's report seems to confirm this.

The 339th Fighter Group Association is still going strong and publishes regular
newsletters. The following article was written by its Editor James R. Starnes (who
was a pilot on this actual mission) and published in the September 1994 edition. The
article is reproduced in full below as it shows graphically that the weather could be
just as great a threat as any enemy could.

> *The Rest of the Story.*　　　　　*Jim Starnes.*　　　　　*505 Sqdn 339th FG.*
> *The mission of 6 Feb. 45 was an escort of B-17s to Bohlen, near Leipzig in eastern
> Germany. I was leading Upper Blue flight on this one when the 505th lost three
> pilots. The group history attributes their loss to weather, which in my opinion is only
> partially accurate. The 505 history scrapbook is even worse in that the summary of the
> loss distorts the way I recall what happened. I would like to describe the mission in
> greater detail after reviewing the written accounts.*

The three squadron mission summary reports show that take-off was about 0850hrs with about 20 aircraft per squadron. The route in was across Holland to rendezvous with B-17s near Dummer Lake in Germany at 25,000ft. Each squadron report says there was a solid undercast all the way, including the target area. At about 12.00hrs the three squadrons broke off escort when we received the mission recall order from 'NUTHOUSE', the ground command station. The 503rd & 504th returned home by a direct route, crossing out near Dunkerque and landing at 14.10 & 14.30 hours. The 505th report states that we made landfall out near Dieppe on the deck and landed at 15.15 hrs. It also states 'Three aircraft not yet returned due to reasons unknown'.

The squadron history summary for Feb. 45 contains the following on their loss: 'On 6th Feb. Cpt. R.W. Bloxham, 1st Lt K.O. Thomas and 2nd Lt G.W. Palmer were MIA after a ramrod (escort) to Bohlen. The trio, it is believed, became lost while crossing the Channel, later spun in. Next day Thomas and Palmer were listed as KIA when, with their aircraft, they were found near Nuthamstead and on the Isle of Wight, respectively. Several days later Bloxham's aircraft was discovered during low tide in the sands off the Isle of Wight, but no trace of his body was found.

For the benefit of those who do not know the location of the Isle of Wight, it is almost 100 miles Southwest of Fowlmere off the south coast of England. What was the 'trio' doing near the Isle of Wight?

They were a 100 miles off course just like the other 16 aircraft in the 505th that day. In my opinion, the official description in those reports amounts to a cover up of a gross navigational error on the part of the formation leader and to a lesser degree of the other four flight leaders, including me.

Let me explain how 19 Mustangs approached the chalky cliffs of the Isle of Wight on the 6 Feb.

When we left the bombers that day, the 505th took a south-westerly heading where the lower clouds were more broken. Like some other pilots in the formation, as blue flight leader I assumed we were diverting around the flak infested Ruhr district of western Germany. However, we continued on a more or less westerly course across France as I grumbled into my oxygen mask 'what are we doing way down here?' The lower clouds had broken up over central France and I could see Rhone River heading south towards Marseilles off our left wing. I finally called Red leader and said we were far south of course and pointed out the terrain features off to the left. He acknowledged the call and made a correction to the right, but not nearly enough to return us to Fowlmere. As we continued Northwest, the upper cloud-deck continued to lower, forcing our formation to gradually descend. Weather continued to deteriorate as visibility dropped along with the bottoms of the clouds. Broken lower clouds obscured any identifying landmarks as we made 'landfall out' at some unknown location in France at fairly low altitude.

Red Leader called 'Gaspump' (Fowlmere Homer) but received no reply. We were too low and too far away. Our five flights closed up, as we were soon right over the waves in order to stay in visual contact with the water. Fog and drizzle made it hard to see ahead as the weather worsened further. After a tense period of minutes over water,

I heard some one call over the radio 'Look out for those cliffs!' I advanced the power smoothly and pulled up into the clouds without even seeing the cliffs.

It was a situation of every flight for itself, and many pilots were unable to hold the formation after an emergency pull-up like that. They went on their own instruments and climbed to a safe altitude. Soon someone called 'Gas pump' for a homing [Signal] and got a reply 'Steer 025 degrees'. By this time only my wingman, Harry Ziegler, was able to stay with me, and he called that he was having problems. I told him to go on his own instruments and believe them rather than his senses.

We took up individual headings of about 025 degrees and using homing calls made it back to Fowlmere where the ceiling was less than 500 feet. Everyone made it safely except the 'Trio' mentioned earlier.

The weather was also to play a major part in the next loss when a Fairey Firefly, serial Z2046, from 798 Sqdn Fleet Air Arm based at Lee on Solent flew into high ground at Chale Green whilst descending through low cloud and fog on the 1st March. The machine, apparently attempting an emergency landing, became the second aircraft to remove part of the roof structure at Northgrounds Farm when it hit the roof of the stable and barn at before crashing into the field on the other side of the road and bursting into flames. Its pilot S/Ldr J.H. Sutton tragically losing his life in this all too common type of crash, his wrecked aircraft being categorised Cat ZZ.

Mustang propellor parts recovered from Puckpool Beach (relates to Bloxham/Palmer incident). (A. T. Gilliam)

Barely six weeks later on 13 April, a Supermarine Sea Otter ABR1, serial JM804 was lost. The amphibious machine attached to the Air Sea Rescue training flight at Eastleigh porpoised during its take off run and capsized into the sea 1½ miles south of the slipway at Lee-on-Solent. Its crew of two suffered different fates; Lt E.C. Soughton tragically lost his life whilst his pilot Lt S. Green scrambled from the wreckage with only minor injuries.

The summer month of June 1945 was to see the next wartime military incident on the Island. On the 27th a Supermarine Walrus I, serial L2335, being operated by No.15 Ferry Pool, lost control during take off from Somerton Airfield and crashed between the Garage and the Scrapyard almost directly opposite the old Aerodrome gate. The amphibian aircraft was being piloted by a young female pilot, Flg-Off A. Walker from the Air Transport Auxiliary. Personnel from the airfield raced to the scene, dragging her clear of the burning wreckage. Later, upon sending flowers to her during her Hospital sojourn they reputedly discovered that she was the daughter of the Johnny Walker Whisky family. The aircraft itself was one of a batch built at Supermarine's Southampton facility at Woolston between 1937 and 1939 and had been originally delivered to the Admiralty before passing to 276 Sqdn RAF in 1943 and then finally to the Ferry pool. After a long flying career, by wartime standards, its final resting-place was to be barely ten miles from its birthplace

The winter 1995 edition of the *W.P.I. Journal**, (the Alumni magazine of the Worcester Polytechnic Institute of Massachusetts) carried a fascinating report of an American's lifelong search for the location of the crash site of one of his closest friends. Part of the article is reproduced below with additional information supplied to me by Nils Askman.

> *In the summer of 1945 a twin-engined plane fell from the sky and crashed at the edge of a cornfield on the Isle of Wight. The pilot, a young American major in the Army Air Force was killed instantly. From the next field, a farmer watched in horror as the plane caught fire and exploded.*
>
> *The news was relayed to the pilot's family. His civilian boss sent word to Alumni secretary Herbert Taylor, who reported the death in the W.P.I. Journal. 'EVERETT W. LEACH, fourth graduate of the class to lose his life during the war, Ev Leach was its acknowledged leader. He was elected permanent class president after having served in that capacity during the senior year.*
>
> *Leach was only one of many alumni of the 1930s and 1940s reported dead, missing, or wounded during the war. In those days the journal devoted as many pages to a column called 'From War Theatres' as it did to 'Around Boyton Hill' (the college's location). In 1950 Leach's photograph appeared again in the Journal when he was awarded a posthumous Distinguished Flying Cross. Leach's wife remarried and moved to the West Coast. Another classmate took on his duties as class president and his alumni file was closed and came to rest in the archives of the Institute.*
>
> *One person could not forget Everett Leach. Nils Askman, who had trained with Leach at Standard Oil, was filled with questions about his friend's death. Where exactly did his plane go down? Why was he flying the training plane that day? What happened to his remains?*

American test pilot Everrett Leach lost his life in the crash of airspeed Oxford, NM247, at Havenstreet on 19 July 1945. (Via W.P.I. Journal*)*

Askman and Leach became fast friends when they met in Standard Oil's engineers training course and were later assigned to work in the same department. Both men enlisted in 1941. Although the Army split them up for training, in a happy series of coincidences they found themselves posted to the same locations over and over again through most of the war. Askman's post war career with ESSO took him to Europe, including several assignments to England where he met and married a nurse from the New Forest. While living in England the couple investigated Leach's death, but uncovered very little, since most information was still classified. After Askman's retirement in 1978 they returned to the States, and had more time to devote to their search.

Nils Askman discovered that his friend had been originally interred at a cemetery just outside of London but had been moved back to his hometown of Worcester, Massachusetts in 1948. Mrs Askman eventually inherited her mother's home in the New Forest and during a visit there, neighbours took the Askmans on a tour of the Isle of Wight. Nils was able to search the *Isle of Wight County Press* archives where he found a brief write up in the paper giving the time, date and location of the crash. During a subsequent visit, Nils managed to track down the farmer who had witnessed his friend's fiery death nearly fifty years earlier and who could pinpoint the crash site. His search over, Nils commissioned a plaque dedicated to Leach's memory at a local war memorial shrine, situated above Havenstreet, less than a mile from the crash site.

19 July 1945 was the fateful day when Leach's Airspeed Oxford, NM247, plummeted from the sky. Leach was a test pilot attached to the Empire Test Pilot School at the Aeroplane & Armament Experimental Establishment (A&AEE) Boscombe Down. He had been posted to this country to conduct trials with America's latest jet fighter – the Lockheed Shooting Star – which was on test with Rolls-Royce engines in place of its usual General-Electric ones. The trials were not going well, with weight and balance problems delaying the work.

Leach filled in his time by check flying repaired aircraft. It was for this reason that he had taken off in the Oxford from Boscombe at 11.30hrs that morning to conduct stability trials. The Oxford was at about 3,000ft when it went out of control. The farmer that witnessed the incident watched as Leach fought to recover control of the aircraft and steer it away from the village instead of baling out. The aircraft impacted into a field at the south-east corner of Rowlands Wood at Havenstreet and exploded. The ambulance and fire services were quickly at the scene but Leach had died instantly in the crash.

An official investigation into the incident was convened and its conclusion was that the crash was caused by the loss, in flight, of the port auxiliary fuel tank. Several eyewitnesses reported seeing a large flat object (which some said was on fire) falling free from the aircraft before it crashed. The tank and the metal panel below it were never found at the crash site. Investigation of the wreckage led to the conclusion that a small fire had started within the wing tank bay, probably caused by fuel spillage being ignited by the engine exhaust. This small fire had burned away the fixings for the metal tank mounting straps, allowing the tank to fall out from inside the wing (a similar accident had previously caused the loss of another Oxford). This would have created a serious trim problem; the aircraft went into a series of tight left-hand turns before momentarily going into a vertical dive. The pilot finally managed to attain some degree of control, but it was too late and the aircraft slammed into the field at a fairly flat angle, breaking up totally and leaving a wreckage trail for some 150 yards.

On 31 August a Miles M33 Monitor TT II, serial NP409, crashed into the sea off Fort Victoria at Yarmouth killing Sqdn Ldr K.W.A. Fehler and Lt L.R.V. Hapgood. The Miles Monitor was a twin-engined aircraft (two 1,750hp Wright Cyclone engines), one of a very small total production of twenty (plus two Mk I prototypes) manufactured before further production for both Navy and RAF was cancelled, none of which actually entered official military service. This particular aircraft had been allocated to the Fleet Air Arm but was actually being operated by the Aeroplane & Armament Experimental Establishment (A&AEE) at Boscombe Down where it was undergoing weight and performance trials.

The type had proven unpopular with its test pilots with various faults, the most serious of which was a tendency for fuel leakage in the vicinity of the engine nacelles which could subsequently be ignited by the exhaust flames from the stub type exhaust deflectors.

Another potential problem had appeared in an earlier force-landing of a Monitor when the fittings securing the pilot's seat back fractured injuring the pilot. On the day of the loss of NP409, the aircraft had been tasked to carry out a target towing flight test at a constant speed of 300mph. Some two hours into the flight as the aircraft was off Yarmouth on a westerly heading at around 2,000ft it suddenly rolled, inverted and dived vertically into the sea. The wreckage was never recovered and so the court of enquiry had no firm evidence to pinpoint the cause of the crash, however they were informed about the seat problem and records showed that the pilot's seat in this particular machine had not yet been modified. The court concluded that the most likely cause of the accident was a structural failure to the seat as the result of a high G manoeuvre rendering the pilot unable to control the aircraft.

The penultimate loss of 1945, which occurred on 1 October, was another accident involving a FAA aircraft, this time caused by structural failure. De Havilland Mosquito FB VI, serial RF829, from 709 Sqdn operating out of Thorney Island was carrying out dummy dive bombing attacks over the sea to the east of the Island when its wing tore off as it attempted to pull out of its dive at around 1,500ft. The machine crashed into the sea $4\frac{1}{2}$ miles south-west of the Nab Tower killing Lt J.K. Harrop.

The year's final loss was that of Fairey Swordfish III, NF333, from the Aircraft Torpedo Development Unit based at Gosport. On 11 October it was involved in a mid-air collision at low level over the torpedo ranges with a Bristol Beaufighter, RD750, also from the ATDU; the Swordfish was unable to maintain control and plunged into the Solent. Flg-Off R.F. Holland was injured in the crash; his fellow crewman Cpl Dicks was killed.

This event was the last recorded incident of military aircraft loss to occur on or around the Island during the war years. However, the years of peace that followed were still to provide the Island with a large number of downed aircraft.

Endnote

* Article written by Joan Killough-Miller and reproduced in part by kind permission of the *W.P.I. Journal*

Chapter Six

Post-War Losses

February 1946 to Present Day

The first recorded loss to occur in the years following the outbreak of peace was that of a Short Sunderland GR5 from 302 FTU. The aircraft, serial VB885, hit the sea on 13 February 1946 during a low turn and broke up off Calshot killing ten crewmembers. This was to be the first of many reminders that peacetime flying was not without its dangers.

A de Havilland Mosquito based at Ford airbase in West Sussex (HMS *Peregrine*) was destined to be the next aircraft to tragically prove this point. The machine from 811 Sqdn of the Fleet Air Arm became yet another victim of bad weather when on 23 July 1946 it flew into high ground in thick fog.

The *Isle of Wight County Press* carried the following report:

> *In a sea fog which enveloped the Needles Downs on Tuesday afternoon, a Fleet Air Arm Mosquito aircraft on exercises with the Home Fleet, crashed into the headland, and the pilot Lieut. Charles Horace Buxton, and the observer, Lieut. Kenneth Stickland both belonging to the Naval Air Station at Ford, Sussex, were killed instantly. It was shortly before 3.30 p.m. when the aircraft was heard at Alum Bay flying overhead in fog so thick that the sea was obscured from the sight of anyone standing on the cliffs, and the sound of the crash was the first indication of the disaster. At first it was thought that the crash had occurred at sea and the Yarmouth Lifeboat put out to make a search, but was recalled when the wreckage was found. The aircraft crashed into the cliff top near the roadway leading to the Needles Battery at a spot where the chalk cliffs rise to a height of about 250ft. It was smashed to matchwood by the impact, wreckage being scattered over a wide radius, some remaining on the cliff top and some falling sheer to the beach where one of the engines was subsequently found. Service personnel were quickly on the spot and a National Fire Service appliance attended but was not needed.*

A couple spending their honeymoon in the Sandown area had a narrow escape on the morning of 9 June 1947 when a Harvard trainer from the Fleet Air Arm base at Lee on Solent crashed through a hedge less than 10ft from them. The aircraft from

North American Harvard IIB. (Air Britain)

799 Squadron suffered throttle problems and the crew attempted to glide down for a forced landing, narrowly missing Yaverland church and Manor House. Farm workers and prisoners of war working in the fields ran to assist the airmen before the arrival of the emergency services. The crew comprising Sub-Lts Lygo and Darlington suffered lacerations, concussion and shock were treated at the scene by a Local doctor before being transferred to Ryde Hospital overnight and then transferred to Lee's own sick quarters on the next day. The honeymoon couple were strolling in the area when they saw the low-flying aircraft approach and thinking it was about to make a normal landing had innocently stopped to watch not realising how close to disaster they had been.

The next recorded loss was that of Mk XVI Spitfire, SL553, from 501 Squadron which like the Mosquito also fell victim to bad weather when it failed to return from a sortie during a snowstorm on 21 February 1948. No trace of wreckage was ever found and the aircraft was presumed, from its last known position, to have been lost into the Solent.

Also lost into the sea off the Island (exact date unspecified), although under far more bizarre circumstances, was a Griffon-engined Mk 45 Seafire, the Naval version of the Spitfire. During the late 1940s and early 1950s, extensive trials had been going on with Seafires to determine their strength and suitability for Naval carrier operations and to evaluate developments in carrier equipment. Tests were carried out on land to investigate the survivability of the aircraft and risk to deck crews following contact with the crash barriers now being installed to catch aircraft that failed to pick up the arrester wires on the carrier deck. Running parallel with these tests were catapult launch trials. The first of these were carried out at the Royal Aircraft Establishment at Meadow Gate and involved firing surplus Seafires from rocket assisted catapults. Further trials were carried out at sea utilising the 'advanced steam catapult' that was undergoing development for the next generation of naval fighters.

At first dead weights consisting of ballasted metal tanks were propelled from the front of the carrier's flight decks. Following the success of these initial tests, a more realistic test vehicle was required and surplus Seafire 45s were used.

The first test aircraft had its outer wing panels removed at the wing cannon position and with its engine running the pilotless machine was launched in a tail down attitude by the steam catapult. The aircraft was expected to ditch into the sea a short distance ahead of the carrier. The test engineers had reckoned without the superb aerodynamics of the Spitfire lineage! The Seafire climbed away from the deck and due to its decreased wing span the engine torque set it into a flight path of slowly decreasing circles around the carrier. The Seafire was still airborne some five minutes later and an order was issued to gunnery control to 'shoot down the Seafire'. However before this could be carried out the aircraft entered the water of its own accord.

Five young lads from a local Squadron of the Air Training Corps had a lucky

Extract from the flying log of Air Cadet T. Jennings showing the ill-fated loss of Anson TX214.
(T. Jennings)

90

escape on 14 March 1948 when the aircraft they were flying in suffered a failure of both engines. The incident happened at Somerton airfield where several ATC groups had assembled for air familiarisation flights. The Avro Anson aircraft, TX214, lost all power just as the undercarriage had been retracted and with no time to lower the wheels again belly landed and skidded across the grass to stop just short of the airfield boundary. One of the former cadets on this flight, Mr T. Jennings, recently provided this insight into the accident.

We taxied out to the runway where we waited for a short while, then the pilot taxied the machine back to the fuel bowser and spoke briefly with the pump operator, we then taxied back out to the start point and commenced our take off run. At about 100ft both engines cut out. By this time, the pilot had retracted the wheels and although he tried to lower them again there was insufficient time to do so. The Anson's undercarriage was lowered manually by operating a hand pump and in attempting to do this rapidly the pilot cut his finger; fortunately this was the only injury sustained in the crash. The aircraft skidded across the field coming to rest fairly close to a bungalow situated near the boundary. The pilot and the Cadets remained inside the aircraft until the site emergency vehicles and the Squadron C.O arrived.

Avro Anson, TX214, following its accident at Somerton, 14 March 1948. (Caption on photo states wrong date). (S. Shawyer)

Gloster Meteor F4. (Air Britain)

TX214 survived this crash relatively unscathed and was repaired on site and flown out from Somerton airfield. After a fairly long flying career it was designated as an 'instructional airframe for historical purposes' (serial 7818M) in August 1963 and was transferred to the RAF Museum. Following a brief spell at RAF Henlow it finally moved to Cosford Aerospace Museum where it is currently on display. Mr Jennings still treasures his ATC Flying Logbook showing this incident, and a copy of the relevant page is included in this work.

The Central Fighter Establishment (CFE) had the dubious honour of losing the first of the new generation of jet aircraft to fall in this area when, on 22 April 1949, Meteor F4, serial VT233, was lost into the sea off Thorney Island after being abandoned whilst in an unrecoverable inverted spin.

August 1949 saw a milestone event in the history of Island air losses. On Friday 12 August the first loss of an Island built jet-powered aircraft was to occur at Cowes. The innovative design team at Saunders Roe had developed and built a turbine powered seaplane fighter aircraft, the diminutive Saro SR/A1, nicknamed 'The Squirt'. The single-seat fighter, serial TG271, one of three prototypes, was originally intended for service in the Pacific war zone where land-based air fields were not always available; but hostilities ended before it was ready for service so it had been retained by the company for test and development work.

On this particular day the aircraft was not to be flown by its regular pilot, Geoffrey Tyson, Saunders' chief test pilot, but by the Naval test pilot Capt. Eric 'Winkle' Brown, CBE, DFC, AFC, who had been newly appointed to Saunders the previous day. Brown had a reasonable seaplane experience and was confident about his ability to fly the somewhat unorthodox machine.

Saro SR/A1, serial TG271. Nicknamed 'The Squirt', seen on trials on the Solent prior to its loss off Cowes. (GKN Westland Aerospace)

He was given a run-down of the controls and flying characteristics of the SR/A1 by Tyson and set of for his takeoff run along Cowes Roads. Take-off was never an easy task in this aircraft but Brown experienced no real problems and was soon airborne and engaged in his pre-set flight plan. The flight went well but as Brown lined up to land in the same direction that he had taken off in he was radioed from the patrol/recovery launch and told to land along a direction of ninety degrees to that of take-off due to a shift in the wind. He saw the launch reposition along this new direction and turned to land parallel to it. Brown recounts in his autobiography that for some unknown reason he decided contrary to his normal jet flying practice that he would land with the cockpit hood open.

He touched down at around 100 knots and the aircraft seemed to be running well on the surface of the water when suddenly he spotted a fleeting glimpse of something dark in the water ahead of him. There was a tremendous crack as something hit the underneath of the hull and, as the object was compressed between the hull and the water below, it shot out sideways like a shell from a cannon and ripped the starboard wing float clean off. The starboard wing immediately dipped into the sea and the craft swung violently to starboard, cartwheeled to port and flipped over onto its back. The aircraft skidded along upside down for a further 50yds before coming to rest.

Inside the inverted cockpit Brown had watched the water rushing past and as the aircraft stopped it began to fill. He unfastened his safety harness and tried to exit from the cockpit but found that he was trapped by his parachute harness. After a great struggle he broke free and tried to reach the surface only to find he could not find his way past the wing. Eventually he made his way to the trailing edge of the wing and surfaced. By now Brown was in poor shape and unable even to inflate his life jacket he just managed to gain a finger hold into a drain hole in the fuselage of TG271 before he passed out.

Geoffrey Tyson leapt fully clothed from the launch just as Brown started to sink under the water again and kept him afloat until he could be recovered into the launch. Brown was rushed to Frank James Hospital in East Cowes where his first recollection was 'coming to spouting water like a whale whilst someone was giving me artificial respiration'. Brown made a remarkably quick recovery from his escapade, being considered fit enough for discharge the following morning and proving the point by piloting his own aircraft back to Farnborough the same day.

The crew of the launch reported that, as they approached the upturned wreckage of the machine, they had seen two holes in the bottom of the hull. Apparently a large piece of wood, possibly part of a mast from a dis-masted yacht taking part in the previous week's Cowes Week Regatta, had embedded itself in the hull. Normally one of the duties of the launch would be to patrol the landing/takeoff lane to look for debris such as this, but the sudden wind change together with the fact that the aircraft was carrying insufficient fuel to circle meant that there was no time to sweep the new landing area.

Of the three examples of the SR/A1 built, only one example, TG263, still exists and is on public display at the Southampton Hall of Aviation. TG271 sank immediately after the accident and despite attempts by divers to recover it was never located in the deep and fast flowing water. The third example was lost into the sea in a flying accident off Felixstowe whilst practising for a Battle of Britain air display.

3 November 1949 saw a major peacetime tragedy unfold to the east of the Island when, at around 20.00hrs in good night time visibility, Upwood-based Lancaster I, TW908, from 148 Sqdn collided with Mosquito RL116 from West Malling. All nine crewmen lost their lives in the collision. Both aircraft were on a fighter affiliation training exercise.

St Catherine's lighthouse staff initially raised the alarm and radioed the Ventnor coastguard to report having seen burning debris fall into the sea. The Bembridge and Selsey lifeboats were launched and joined a Swedish merchant vessel, the *Patria*, in a search of the crash area around six miles south of the Nab Tower.

Lookouts on the liner *Queen Mary*, which was inbound to Southampton from New York, reported seeing 50ft flames in the channel off the Island and the Captain ordered the liner to turn back and assist in the search. However once the *Patria* radioed that it had recovered wreckage the *Queen Mary* resumed its original course.

The search vessels had perfect weather for a search, with a flat calm sea and bright moonlight throughout the night, the lifeboats staying on station until around 01.00hrs The surface vessels, whose efforts were assisted by flares dropped from aircraft, recovered a small amount of wreckage. This included an empty dinghy, a main wheel, and the logbook from the Lancaster.

The following day two naval vessels, HMS *Romola* and HMS *Redpole*, resumed the search. The body of Flg-Off A.L. Miller, the Mosquito pilot, was recovered by HMS *Romola*. No other bodies were recovered. The other crewmen to lose their lives in this tragedy were (Lancaster) Flg-Off J. Oldham, D.M. McCall, L.H. Stephens, E.G. Clarke, S. Mason, G.J. Chapman, W. Meldrum, (Mosquito) Navigator Flt Lt E.C. Daigety.

An interesting personal element to this incident is contained in the autobiography of Captain H. Grattidge, who was the captain of the *Queen Mary* on the night of this incident. In his book *Captain of the Queens* he relates firstly, the details of the night's incident and then goes on to say how, months later, he was asked by a close friend to do a favour.

His friend rang him to say that he had been talking to a girl who worked in one of the kiosks aboard the great liner, and that she would very much like to have a personal word with the captain. He added that as she was a very shy person, and in deference to his position, it would be better if he approached her. Having described where and how to find her, and getting the captain's word that he would contact her, he rang off.

Grattidge was intrigued and set out to locate the young lady. She blushed slightly when he introduced himself; Grattidge was still unaware as to why she wished to speak to him. She spoke quietly, 'It was only that I wanted to see you and thank you for trying to rescue those flyers off Southampton in November.' Grattidge replied that any ship would have done the same. 'Perhaps,' she replied, 'but you see, when her husband is one of the pilots involved, a wife sees it differently.' The captain could not remember his exact reply, but he tried to convey how he felt about her working aboard ship, powerless to help, as her husband perished so close by. 'But I wasn't,' she replied, 'I was working in London at the time. I was in another job. But when I heard what the *Queen Mary* had tried to do, I knew there was only one place in the world that I could work after that'. Grattidge was deeply touched by this and commented that her words were a greater reward than any he had received in more than forty years at sea.

Barely five months elapsed before another jet aircraft was to fall in this area. On 29 March 1950 Meteor F4, VW277, from 56 Squadron flew into the Mudflats off Thorney Island Airbase whilst practising formation aerobatics.

'Flying tragedy at Ryde, Naval plane crashes in road, Both occupants killed'. These were the headlines from Saturday 11 November *Isle of Wight County Press*. The previous Tuesday (7 November 1950), a de Havilland Tiger Moth, serial BB865, from the Fleet Air Arm base, HMS Siskin, at Gosport had crashed in High Park Rd, Ryde, killing its two occupants and narrowly missing two young girls playing on the other side of the road. The accident happened at around 15.20hrs The aircraft had been performing aerobatics over the Elmfield area of Ryde when it seemed to get into difficulties, failed to recover from a low level loop and plunged into the residential street from about 150ft. It fell partly on the pavement and partly onto a hedge bordering a vacant plot adjacent to a house called 'The Kyles'. As the aircraft crashed it brought down telephone lines, tore branches from surrounding trees and demolished the gate and fence of 'the Kyles'.

A lamppost and a telegraph pole finally arrested the machine's path. Wreckage was hurled right across the street and the plane was totally destroyed. Police and Fire services were on the scene within minutes, but luckily the wreckage did not catch

Fairey Firefly F1 on display at the RAF Museum Hendon. (Air Britain)

fire. The emergency services cut the crew from the wreckage but nothing could be done for them. The pilot had been Lt Edward Kierman, an experienced flyer with over nine hundred hours in his logbook. The passenger was a civilian airframe engineer on contract to the Navy from Westland Aircraft Ltd. An inquest held at Ryde the following week returned an accidental death verdict on the two flyers but despite much speculation could not shed any light on what had caused the crash.

The start of 1951 saw another Naval machine come down in the Ryde area. Fortunately the only fatality in this incident was a grazing cow. At around mid-day on Monday 21 January Fairey Firefly IV, TW738, suffered a complete engine failure and force-landed at East Ashey Manor Farm on the outskirts of Ryde. The aircraft was from 771 Sqdn based at Ford airfield near Worthing. The machine touched down in a field before skidding through a hedge and hitting a tree and the unfortunate cow. Two housewives from nearby cottages had heard the crash and ran to scene to find that the aircraft had come to rest at the base of the tree. The crew, comprising of Lt J.F. Tuttle USN and Lt D. Duncan RN, had suffered only fairly minor injuries and were exiting from the wreckage as the ladies arrived. Police and fire services were quickly on the scene, but thankfully the Firefly did not catch fire. The two crewmen were conveyed to Ryde County Hospital where their injuries were attended to before they were taken to Ryde Airport for the short helicopter ride back to their Sussex base.

*Fairey Firefly, WD920, following forced landing at Sandown Marshes, 22 November 1953.
(J. Casford)*

Part of the cockpit canopy from WD920 recovered from the marshes. Currently on display at Bembridge Heritage Centre. (A.T. Gilliam)

Sunderland Flying Boat in flight over the Isle of Wight. (C. Dover)

Another large flying boat came to grief in the Solent on 16 November 1951 when a Short Sunderland V, serial SZ565, from 235 Operational Conversion Unit (OCU) crashed whilst landing off Hillhead (near Lee on Solent) and sank.

The first of two accidents in March 1953 involved Avro Anson T21, serial VV900 from No.2 Air Navigation School which on the 13th of that month undershot a night landing at RAF Thorney Island and crashed short of the airfield onto the mudflats that surround the island airbase at low tide. The Anson was damaged beyond repair in the force-landing.

The Air Services Training Establishment (ASTE) based at Hamble on Southampton Water was the operator of the next aircraft to end its career on the Island. ASTE were under government contract to train military pilots of various nationalities. On Sunday 22 March 1953 a civilian registered Chipmunk, G-AMUD operated by ASTE crash landed at Porchfield killing its Malayan pilot, Mr M. Thiyagajah and seriously injuring its passenger Mr I.P. Fernandes, who was an Indian student pilot.

The aircraft had taken off from Hamble at 11.05hrs, proceeded to the Island to practise spinning, stalling, steep turns, and forced landing approaches to Cowes Aerodrome. Shortly before the accident the pilot had climbed to 6,500ft to practise spin recovery. At around 11.20hrs the aircraft was seen flying low in the Porchfield

Sunderland Flying Boat. (Air Britain)

Sunderland Flying Boat on the slipway at Calshot. (C. Dover)

area, shortly afterwards the Chipmunk was seen to enter a left-hand spin, making several revolutions before it flew into the ground. The machine struck the ground with little forward speed with its wings level and in a slightly nose down attitude. The propeller was undamaged suggesting that the machine was not under power at the moment of impact. The inquiry determined that the crash occurred due to the pilot losing control of the aircraft though no reason as to why he had lost control could be established; the passenger had no recollection of the crash and therefore could offer no explanation. The board commented that both occupants had sustained head injuries as a result of their heads coming into contact with the instrument panels, with the safety harnesses correctly adjusted there should be a clearance of at least 9in between the panels and a fully forward head position. It would seem that if the straps had been adequately tensioned these injuries would not have occurred.

Later that year two more aviators had a much luckier arrival onto Island soil. On 21 November 1953 Sub-Lt P. Metcalf & Lt E.B.O. Smith (the pilot and observer) of the Channel Air Division, Royal Naval Volunteer Reserve, stepped unhurt from their Fairey Firefly, serial WD920, after it force-landed near Browns Golf Course at Sandown following engine failure. Damage to the aircraft was limited to a bent propeller and to the underside of the fuselage. The aircraft, from the Head Quarters of the Channel Air Division based at Ford airfield in Sussex, was recovered and taken to R.N.A.Y. Fleetlands (Gosport) for repair. Part of the cockpit canopy from this aircraft was subsequently found on the marshes and is on display at the Bembridge Heritage Centre.

Just before 11.00hrs on Thursday 8 December 1955, Sqdn Ldr David Dick was test flying Gloster Javelin Mk I, serial XA561, at 45,000ft. Over the Island when during spinning trials the aircraft entered a 'Super Stall'★ condition from which it would not recover.

Despite considerable effort by Sqdn Ldr Dick to regain some sort of control over the aircraft, the situation soon became untenable and he was forced to eject at around 6,000ft, drifting safely to earth near the old cement mill on Brading Marshes. The proprietor of Wall Lane Garage and two colleagues set off in a four-wheel drive vehicle across the marshes to collect the pilot, but within ten minutes Lee on Solent's air sea rescue helicopter had put down alongside the pilot.

In the mean time the doomed jet had crashed at Rowborough Corner, near the T-junction of the Ryde - Brading road and the St Helens road. The aircraft had come down in a basically flat attitude with very little forward speed and had impaled itself virtually intact on an Oak tree and some fence posts.

The nearby Rowborough Cottage was almost certainly saved from damage by the tree because it swung the wreckage around as it impacted; the nose of the machine coming to rest no more than 15ft from the cottage. Parts of the aircraft were jammed against the Southern Electricity Board's electrical sub-station; two fitters who were due to have been working inside had a lucky escape because they were running late that morning.

Local fire and rescue services were quickly on the scene to deal with the fire that had broken out. The ASR helicopter was put down close to the site so that Sqdn Ldr Dick could assure the fire brigade that no one remained in the aircraft. The

Javelin was a fairly large twin engined aircraft with a wing span of 52ft and a fuselage length of 56ft. Its wreckage blocked the road completely for forty-eight hours, single lane traffic was flowing by the Saturday but it was not until the following Friday that the crash examiners had finished their work and the road was back to normal. The gnarled and blackened tree stump remained at the site long after all other traces of the crash had been cleared away.

At the time of the incident the aircraft was being operated by the A&AEE at Boscombe Down and the Sqdn Ldr was involved in an extensive test programme of new jet fighter aircraft. The prototype Javelin (WD804) had first flown barely four years earlier on 26 November 1951 and had crashed some seven months later following the in-flight loss of both its elevators. Much research was still going on in the field of high speed jet aircraft design and in order to gain as much insight as possible into every aspect of this Sqdn Ldr Dick's test pilot training ensured that he transmitted a running commentary of the spin for as long as possible before ejecting. The resulting tape of the incident is apparently regarded as something of a classic.

Sqdn Ldr Dick's career continued satisfactorily after this incident, he carried on with 'A' Squadron at Boscombe until 1957, followed by two ground tours and command of a V Bomber squadron before returning to Boscombe as Superintendent of Flying. This was followed by several other postings including two Whitehall stints and a return

Gloster Javelin FAW1: All weather interceptor. (Air Britain)

Gloster Javelin XA561, crash-landed onto Rowborough Junction, Brading, 8 December 1955 after its pilot was forced to eject. Note the small building (electricity sub-station) in the lower left of the photo. (Air Vice Marshal Dick)

to Boscombe as Commandant. David Dick retired from the RAF in 1979 as Air Vice Marshall Dick CB. CBE. AFC. MA. FRAeS and has kindly adapted the following narrative from an article written by him in 1992 for inclusion in this work. The section included below outlines the test flying regime of the Javelin in general and includes a fascinating insight into the events immediately preceding the Brading crash:

> *My main project was the Javelin, which started its clearance trials in 1955. It was delayed because three aircraft had been lost during the firm's development programme. Two test pilots were killed; one had entered a spin and the pilot made an unsuccessful ejection; the other was lost without trace, but was also thought to have entered a spin. Thus when the Javelin finally arrived at Boscombe it was not with the happiest reputation.*
>
> *In the light of its troubles, extensive wind tunnel and model dropping tests had offered some understanding of the likely behaviour in a spin. Wing Commander 'Dicky' Martin, DFC AFC RAF (Retd), who had recently been appointed chief test pilot at Glosters then successfully carried out a remarkable – and hazardous – investigative flight test programme for which he deserves the greatest credit. The programme centred around Mk. 1 aircraft XA548, with XA561 as reserve. Both were fitted with a spin recovery parachute, and XA548 had extensive flight test instrumentation. In the summer of*

1955 Dicky Martin carried out many spins on XA548, and demonstrated that a spin always followed a stall, and that there had been consistent behaviour. So two of us from 'A' Squadron assessed it at Boscombe Down confirming Gloster's findings.

The behaviour was unique. Before entering a spin there was a sudden reversal of lateral and directional stability. Control had been lost; the nose would then rise up and speed fell off rapidly; the rudder would move itself fully over in one direction and the aircraft would yaw accordingly, but roll in the opposite direction. After a pause with the IAS (indicated air speed) 'off the clock' it would then spin.

No two spins were identical, and it was seldom possible to enter a spin in any particular direction; the Javelin determined the direction of spin! The oscillatory spin was not violent; the rate of rotation was slow – about one turn in seven or ten seconds. The nose pitched up and down, often through as much as 70 degrees. As the nose rose, the rates of yaw and roll decreased and sometimes stopped altogether as the nose reached its highest point; as the nose pitched down again the rates increased sharply as the aeroplane yawed and rolled into the spin once more. Often in mid spin, when the nose was at its highest position, the Javelin would decide to reverse the direction of rotation; this was heralded by the rotation ceasing momentarily, the rudder slamming fully over in the opposite direction and the aircraft rolling sharply into a spin the other way. In the spin Dicky Martin had recommended holding the stick fully back and central; the rudder forces being extremely heavy, and it was left to do its own thing throughout the spin; it would position itself fully in the direction of rotation.

Recovery action had to be taken at the optimum moment – immediately the nose started to pitch down from its high position. With the control column right back, full aileron had to be applied in the same direction as the spin. The control column was then moved sharply right forward, still keeping on the full aileron. The rudder was still left alone. This action seldom had any immediate effect, but nevertheless these actions were maintained, and if the direction of rotation reversed, the control column still had to be held fully forward, but moved over into the corner of the new spin direction and held there.

When the Javelin decided to stop spinning, it would do so after the nose was at its low point in the pitching cycle. Usually the rotation would cease and the aeroplane would hang in a nose down attitude for a second or two – but this was a trap! Centralising the controls at this point would lead to the aircraft re-entering a spin. The control column had to be held in the fully forward corner until the aircraft did a quite unmistakable sharp nose down pitch – minus $2\frac{1}{2}$ 'g' was a typical value. Once the Javelin had shaken off the spin in this way then recovery was complete; the IAS rose rapidly, the controls could be centralised and the aircraft eased out of the dive. Naturally, there was a large loss of height and recovery by 15,000ft was essential.

Thus the central problem of the Javelin was that there was always much less natural warning of an impending stall than on previous night fighters; that a spin always followed a stall; the inevitable spin was highly unconventional, as were the spin recovery actions. Assuming that all Javelin spins were like those of XA548, the A&AEE's concern was twofold: whether the behaviour at the stall-plus-spin was acceptable for pilots to be trained to do, and then to be able to carry out regularly, including recovery on instruments; and perhaps more importantly – whether, in service *use, the natural stall warning was adequate for fighter pilots to avoid inadvertently spinning – especially off turning flight at high altitude when both the indicated airspeeds and engine thrusts were low.*

We could reach agreement on the second point, and it was therefore decided that to get three more opinions we would convert three more 'A' Squadron test pilots to spin the Javelin, using the reserve aeroplane XA561. Because all the spinning tests had been done on XA548, I carried out a check flight on 561 on the 8 December 1955. I did three spins; the first two were similar to those experienced on XA548. On entering the third spin of this flight, off a spiral turn at 42,000ft at 240 knots IAS, I entered a spin which was utterly different from all the others.

It was smooth and flat. I described the whole event into the voice recorder, and took all the actions, which we had rehearsed in the event of such a situation, but none had any effect. I knew it was vital to get some information back, and I passed three radio messages to Boscombe to let them know of my problem. At about 20,000ft I streamed the spin recovery parachute, but it did not fill because there was no wind outside! When I saw the altimeter pass 15,000ft it was time to go. After a quick 'mayday' call, as I was near the sea, I jettisoned the useless spin recovery chute, as I did not want to be fielded by it. I then pulled the handle which ejected first the cockpit canopy and then me.

An intensive programme to develop and prove a stall warning system was given a high priority. The RAEs Aero Flight, The Institute of Aviation Medicine, Glosters and A&AEE were all involved. Activated by a pair of electro-mechanical vanes on each wing, an unmistakable duplicated two-stage audio warning, which could not be muted, was fitted to all subsequent Javelins. Pilots were cleared to pull into the buffet as far as the first stage warning; the second stage warning, set further into the buffet but still leaving a safe margin from real trouble, signalled an emergency demanding that the pilot must immediately push the stick sharply forward. A&AEEs programme to prove its safety, reliability and effectiveness involved hundreds of spiral dives, covering every corner of the flight envelope up to 45,000ft and Mach 0.95, was done at all realistic loadings, by two pilots and, to ensure that the results were not particular to one aeroplane, on two fully instrumented Mk 4 Javelins. The results were successful and, especially in its later marks the Javelin served successfully in many theatres. It was the RAF's first fighter which pilots were not permitted to stall.

The *Isle of Wight County Press* for Saturday 16 March 1957 carried the tragic heading: JET PILOT KILLED NEAR YARMOUTH. AIRCRAFT EXPLODES AND DISINTEGRATES. The article went on to describe how Hawker Hunter XF427 from 54 Squadron based at RAF Odiham near Alton had been totally destroyed three days earlier when it ploughed into a field just a couple of hundred yards north of the main Newport to Yarmouth road at Bouldner. The crash happened at 15.05hrs creating a crater measuring 40ft by 30ft and some 15ft deep from which smoke continued to issue until dusk. Wreckage and huge lumps of clay, some weighing as much as 3cwt, was scattered over an area of approximately a quarter of a mile, with large amounts dropping vertically down onto the road whilst smaller debris particles scythed horizontally through the hedgerows bordering the road. Neighbouring buildings were extensively

Hawker Hunter F6. (Air Britain)

damaged, one large piece of burning debris fell onto the roof of a barn at Lucketts farm but was quickly dealt with by a local farmer who, having arrived on the scene almost immediately after the impact, bravely clambered onto the roof and knocked it clear. The occupants of the cottage known as Lucketts on the opposite side of the road to the farm buildings escaped uninjured when clay 'bombs' crashed through their roof, wrecking the northern side of the roof and punching holes up to 2ft in diameter in other parts of the roof. A small row of trees between the crash site and the property probably saved the cottage and its occupants from further destruction.

Several people had been at work in the fields and copses close by and were able to give graphic accounts of the Hunter's last moments. Two Forestry Commission workers had been working near to Bouldner cliffs when their attention was aroused by the noise of a fast approaching aircraft. They then saw what they described as the shadow of an aircraft through the cloud, which they estimated, was 200–300ft high. The aircraft was approaching from the direction of Lymington and they thought that the engine did not sound right. One of the workers told the Coroners Court that he said to his companion 'Look out, this things not right, we have got to take cover, it's going to crash.' They threw themselves to the ground and seconds later there was an explosion and a fireball. Visibility was around 500-600yds at the time and they never saw the aircraft come clear of the cloud. The machine impacted approximately a quarter of a mile from where they had been working.

Another eye witness had been working in a small copse some 600yds to the south of the crash site and on hearing the approach of the machine ceased work and tried to look for it. He was looking towards the crash site as it impacted and caught a mere glimpse of it hitting the ground before it was consumed by the explosion. He added that the engine note appeared to be changing as though the aircraft was coming out of a dive and was attempting to climb again.

Fire appliances from Yarmouth and Freshwater were quickly on the scene accompanied by an ambulance, police cars, a rescue helicopter from RAF Thorney Island and soldiers from nearby Golden Hill Fort; but very little could be done. Fire from the burning wreckage and the fuel soaked ground had been extinguished by local farm workers; the pilot Flt Lt Michael Adrian Crook had died instantly. All that could be done was to search for and make safe live ammunition that was scattered across the area and to commence the gruesome task of recovering the shattered remains of Flt Lt Crook and remove them to Yarmouth mortuary.

The inquest heard that twenty-eight-year-old Flt Lt Crook was a pilot of some four years experience who had amassed 268 hours of flying hours in Hunters and was considered an extremely capable pilot. The aircraft itself was fairly new, having logged only twenty hours of flight time and squadron records showed it had been certified serviceable that day at 10.40hrs for an earlier flight and again at 12.30hrs for the fateful flight. The Hunter had carried sufficient fuel for the sortie and maintenance records for the preceding six weeks had shown no known defects or problems.

The Hunter had taken off from Odiham that afternoon for a height climb and aerobatic exercise. No set course was given for the sortie and Flt Lt Crook was asked to provide a weather report to the west of the normal operating area for sorties of this type. There was a weather front approaching from the south-west and Crook radioed a report at 14.36hrs as he passed over Andover and another over Selsey at 14.42hrs This report was transmitted on the airfields approach frequency and was partly garbled. Replaying the tape following the crash the air traffic controller discerned the message as 'Odiham 13. Selsey weather, four-eighths, visibility five miles.' No further transmissions were heard from XF427.

The Coroner returned a verdict of misadventure saying that the aircraft was flying very near the ground in cloud and that the pilot would have been unable to see where he was going. He went on to say that it was for the RAF Board of Enquiry to establish if possible the exact reason for this incident and expressed his sympathy to the pilot's relatives, adding that this was sometimes the price which had to be paid for flying fast aircraft: a point which is unfortunately still relevant today.

On 28 March 1957 the Fleet Air Arm's 831 Sqdn lost two aircraft. The Westland Wyvern S.4's, WL887, & WP343, had taken off from West Sussex's Ford airfield on a one-hour sortie to practice quarter angle attacks on each other. Both machines disappeared over Bracklesham Bay and are presumed to have collided, both pilots tragically losing their lives in the process.

At around 13.40hrs on 29 March 1966 de Havilland Chipmunk G-ARME from the Hamble College of Air Training failed to recover from a spin and crashed half a mile to the west of Adgestone, near Sandown, killing its trainee pilot. The aircraft departed from Hamble airfield at 13.05hrs on a solo training flight that was intended to cover various landing procedures at both Hamble and Lee on Solent. The pilot, nineteen-year-old Mr G.G. Stewart, had been instructed to carry out touch and go landings at Lee and return to Hamble no later than 13.45hrs. After successfully completing three touch and go landings at Lee the machine left the Lee circuit at 13.24hrs and made no further radio contact.

Between 13.35hrs and 13.50hrs the pilot of a Naval Seahawk was overflying the Sandown area at 3,000ft and saw the Chipmunk off to his port side and about 100ft below his flight level. The pilot of the faster Seahawk increased his altitude slightly to ensure there would be no risk of a collision.

Around this time a ground witness saw the Chipmunk commence a right hand spin from an estimated height of 3,000ft, the spin was observed to flatten out and at around 1,500ft a burst of engine noise was heard briefly before dying away without any apparent effect on the machines' spin. There was no witness to the actual impact but two people who had seen the aircraft spin down behind a low hill realised that it had no chance of recovery and quickly made their way towards the scene where they found the wreckage with the pilot unconscious but alive. Before they could open the cockpit to remove the pilot they had to straighten the rear fuselage which was almost severed from the rest of the craft. However the pilot had sustained severe spinal injuries and several skull fractures and despite every effort died from his injuries several hours later.

The machine had hit the ground in a slightly nose down attitude with virtually no forward speed, coming to rest straddling a barbed wire fence. The fuselage had been virtually severed in two and the undercarriage mounts were forced upwards through the top wing skinning. The decking between the two cockpits which carries the mounting for the front cockpit harness had torn away from its mountings allowing the pilot's head to travel far enough forward to impact the instrument panel.

Student pilot Stewart had approximately 150 hours of flying in his log book and was assessed as average in flying ability under normal circumstances but not to have sufficient ability to react adequately under high work load situations. Due to his poor progress he had already had a special check flight with an instructor that morning which had not gone too well and he had been advised that he could soon be off the course if his ability did not improve. The aircraft had been acquired from the RAF in 1961 and at the time of the accident was well maintained with no known defects and operating well within its weight limits and subsequent inspection revealed there had been no pre-crash failures nor were there any loose items in the cockpit which could have jammed the controls.

The enquiry found no conclusive reason for the crash but noted several points; the crash site is fifteen miles from the Hamble and therefore the Chipmunk could not have returned to base by the briefed time. Hamble's standing orders state that students may only carry out exercises for which they have been briefed. Why Stewart was over the Island will never be known but perhaps his mental attitude had been affected by the chastisement following the earlier check flight. Stewart commenced his spin from around 3,000ft when Hamble College's training recommended a starting height for spinning of at least 6,000ft. They added that the possibility that a turbulent wake from the Seahawk had caused the pilot of the Chipmunk to lose control and enter the spin could not be discounted.

Wednesday 26 June 1968 saw Vickers-Supermarine Scimitar, serial XD236 engaged on radar trials with naval shipping to the south of St Catherine's Point. Around lunchtime eye witness reports claimed that the machine was seen to approach from the direction of the sea, low and on fire, and that as it turned to avoid the mist covered St Catherine's Down there was a loud explosion. The aircraft was a Fleet Air Arm machine on loan to Airwork Ltd at the Fleet Requirement Unit based at Bournemouth (Hurn) Airport in Dorset. Its civilian pilot was a young but experienced (ex RAF) Terence Edgar Hill of Wimborne.

A reconstruction of the course probably taken by Mr Hill showed that instead of using the usual route for aircraft test flights to the south of St Catherine's lighthouse he veered slightly northwards in the mist and, after striking the top of a wall adjacent to the private road leading to the radio installations on the top of the Down, the aircraft careered out of control and in flames down the side of the hill towards Niton. The stricken machine then collided with overhead power lines causing the explosion that was reported by many of the eyewitnesses.

The Scimitar was completely destroyed in the crash and subsequent fire. The fuselage ended up no more than ten feet from the main Niton to Blackgang road. Other smaller pieces of debris covered a large area and the badly burned body of the unfortunate Mr Hill was found along with his seat some 400yds away at the base of

Supermarine Scimitar F1. (Air Britain)

109

the Downs. Despite the problems created by the loss of power in the area caused by the impact with the power lines and the consequential loss of radio communications for the Police and Fire Brigade, the emergency services were soon on the scene. In fact the first to arrive must have been either a local police motorcycle-patrolman who was actually following a bus through Niton at the time of the crash; or the local village Police officer whose house was virtually opposite to the crash site and who had watched the burning aircraft as it seemed to hurtle directly at his home.

At first confusion as to the type of aircraft that had crashed led to an air and sea search by Naval vessels, the Bembridge Lifeboat and helicopters from Lee-on-Solent, for other crew members, which was called off once it was established that the incident involved only one single seat aircraft. Personnel from the Naval air station at Lee-on-Solent (HMS *Daedalus*) mounted an overnight guard on the wreckage until experts could arrive the following day from the Fleet Air Arm's accident investigation unit to begin the painstaking task of finding the cause of the tragedy.

The subsequent inquest was held 'in camera' so that very little detail could be obtained from that source. The court of enquiry gave pilot error as the cause for the accident although there were views that the local radio positioning aids that the pilot was tuned to were at that time a little unreliable and could have been partly to blame for the collision. A colleague of the pilot from the Fleet Requirements unit told me that had Mr Hill been just 100yds further south he would have been frightened but would have otherwise survived a very near accident.

'Fog hinders search for the pilot of missing jet' was the headline to a report in the *Isle of Wight County Press* of 2 November 1984. The report went on to detail how the Bembridge Lifeboat had returned to base just before midnight on Wednesday 31 October after searching in vain for nearly eight hours for the pilot of a Hawker Hunter that had crashed into the sea off Sandown.

This incident bore a close resemblance to the Scimitar crash at Niton sixteen years earlier. Once again an ex RAF civilian pilot, Mr Leonard E. Clowes from Marnhull in Dorset, working for the Fleet Requirement and Direction Unit (FRADU) now based at RNAS Yeovilton had crashed in mist whilst on Fleet Radar Trials. The low flying Hunter vanished from radar screens at about 15.30hrs after entering a bank of sea fog and was believed to crashed into the sea five miles south of Langstone Harbour. HMS Glasgow was in charge of the subsequent sea search along with several Minesweepers helicopters, hovercraft, Bembridge and Selsey Lifeboats and six fishing boats. The fog severely hampered the search, visibility being down to 50yds at times. Pieces of wreckage and the pilot's flying helmet were recovered from the sea some two miles from the Nab Tower. The air and sea search was resumed the following day. This aircraft was a T.8C variant of the Hunter, serial XL584, and had enjoyed quite a career. Prior to its use by FRADU it had been based at RNAS Yeovilton where it had been the personal aircraft of the Flag Officer, Naval Aviation.

I personally have a vivid recollection of this incident. That particular day I was working as an electrician at a house close to Bembridge Airport. I remember it being a fairly bright day for the time of year and I was working outside the premises installing lighting along a perimeter wall. I had heard the Hunter making several low passes through the Sandown Bay area and having watched similar trials whilst working in Sandown and having a keen interest in aircraft I was listening intently and trying to visualise the flight path of the aircraft. On the last fly past the high pitched whine of the aircraft's turbine was suddenly replaced by a loud dull thud followed by an eerie silence. Before very long the silence was replaced by the sounds of several two-tone horns from the various emergency services and by the clatter of helicopter rotors as they searched to and fro just off the coast. I went inside and said to my fellow worker that I was sure that I had just heard an aircraft crash into the sea.

At the time of writing, this incident was the last of over 300 military air losses in and around the Isle of Wight.

Endnote

* 'Super Stall' is a nose high, low forward speed flight condition peculiar to certain aircraft designs, notably the high T-tailed, Delta wing planform of the Javelin.

Chapter Seven

Destroyed, Demobbed, Deliberated On

Miscellaneous Losses and Rumours

Throughout the long research process for this book several types of incidents have come to light which although not strictly within the realms of the main body of the book have been considered worthy of inclusion in their own separate chapter. As the chapter name suggests there are three such categories:

Destroyed: Aircraft destroyed by enemy action whilst they were under construction on the Island.

Demobs: Ex-Military aircraft which had been sold and converted to civilian usage and have subsequently crashed in the area.

Deliberated on: Incidents which have been related to the author by witnesses but which have not been corroborated from other sources and records due to insufficient detail. Any further information on these 'Rumour Mill' incidents would be particularly pleasing.

Into the first of these categories come seven Supermarine Walrus amphibians. These were all Mk I machines; part of a batch of sixty-five being manufactured at Saunders Roe's Somerton works under contract No.B43393/39. The aircraft concerned were: X9499, X9518, X9525, X9554, X9557, X9558, X9560; all of which are recorded as being Taken on Charge (TOC) at Saro in May 1942 but never subsequently delivered. They are assumed to have been destroyed in the heavy bombing raids which caused considerable damage both to the Somerton Works and to the outskirts of Cowes during the night of 4/5 May 1942.

The second category opens with the loss of Avro Anson type 652A, civilian registration G-AHFV, which was lost into the sea at a position estimated to be some fifteen miles S.S.W. of Brook at around 10.40hrs on 3 July 1947. The machine,

Crash map G-AHFV

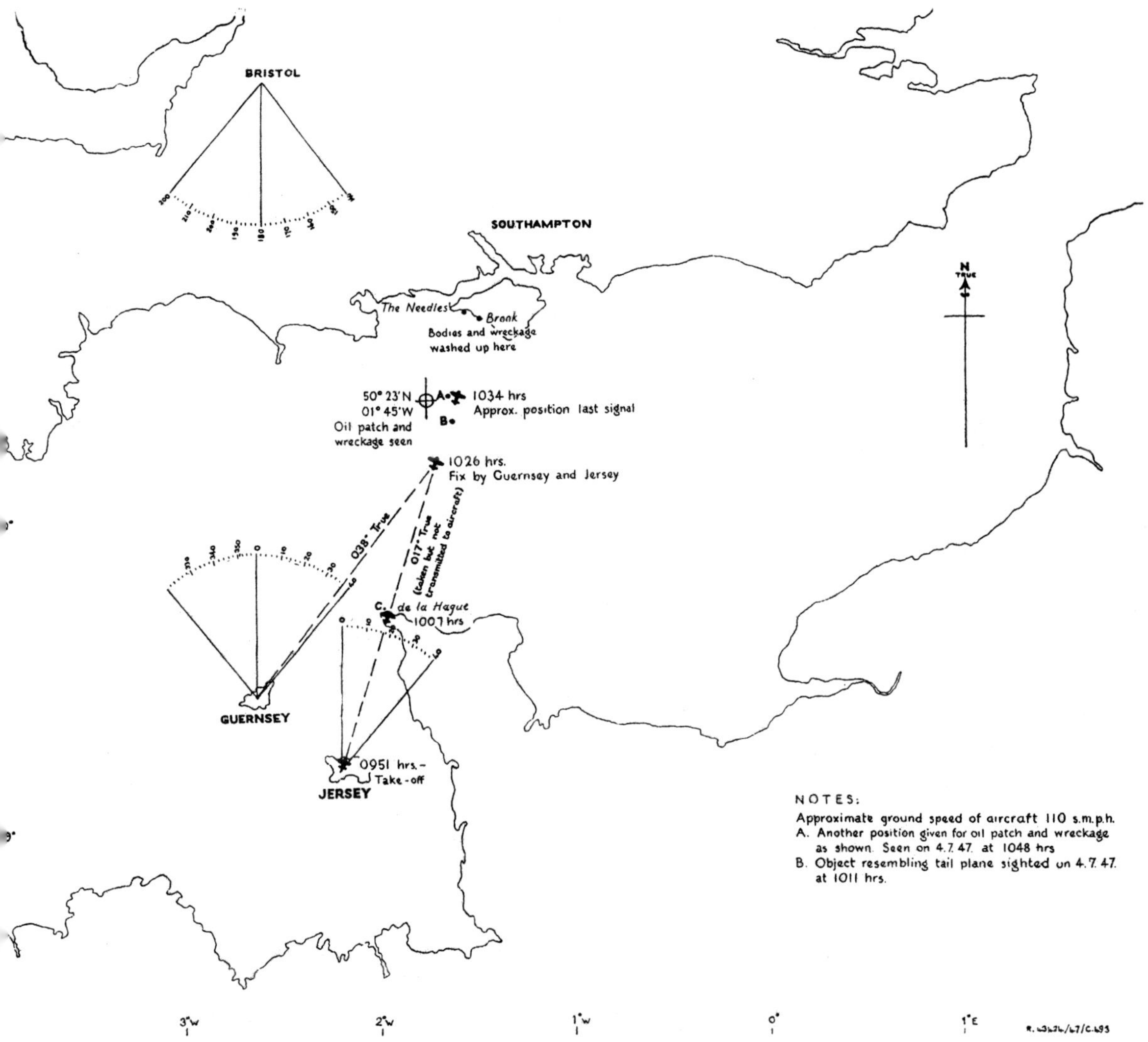
BRISTOL
SOUTHAMPTON
The Needles
Brook
Bodies and wreckage washed up here
50° 23'N
01° 45'W
Oil patch and wreckage seen
A
B
1034 hrs
Approx. position last signal
1026 hrs.
Fix by Guernsey and Jersey
038° True
017° True (taken but not transmitted to aircraft)
C. de la Hague
1007 hrs
GUERNSEY
0951 hrs. – Take-off
JERSEY
N
TRUE
NOTES:
Approximate ground speed of aircraft 110 s.m.p.h.
A. Another position given for oil patch and wreckage as shown. Seen on 4.7.47. at 1048 hrs
B. Object resembling tail plane sighted on 4.7.47. at 1011 hrs.
3°W
2°W
1°W
0°
1°E

formerly serial AW996, had been purchased from the RAF in June 1946 by Southampton Air Services Ltd and completely overhauled and converted for civilian use by them before being sold to Air Transport Association Ltd in June 1947. Records show that since the overhaul no major defects had occurred and all routine maintenance and inspections had been satisfactorily carried out. At the time of the accident the machine's total time in air was 1,815 hours.

The Anson, which had already completed a charter flight between Guernsey and Jersey that morning, took off at 09.51hrs from Jersey airport for a positioning flight to Southampton airport (Eastleigh) where it was due to undertake another charter. At 10.07 the aircraft called Eastleigh and the pilot gave his position as Cap-Le-Hague, height 3,000ft. and estimated time of arrival (ETA) as 10.55hrs. At 10.12hrs Eastleigh was requested to give visibility and cloud extent and height at the airport and these were passed to the Anson; interestingly the barometric pressure at the airport (used for setting the altimeter) was neither requested nor given. The general weather forecast for the Island area at 10.00hrs that morning was: Overcast with patches of sea fog in the Channel, cloud 10/10 at 300 to 500ft, visibility generally four-six miles below cloud but reducing to 500yds or less in fog patches.

As is the customary practice, the information was repeated back from the aircraft to the airport control at 10.20hrs. Six minutes later G-AHFV called Guernsey control and requested a QTE report (what is my true bearing from your location) and this was passed as 138 degrees. At 10.29hrs Eastleigh was called again but could not respond because they were working another aircraft and G-AHFV was asked to wait. At 10.32hrs Eastleigh heard the Anson trying to contact Bristol Control, at 10.34hrs Bristol acknowledged the call, repeated the aircraft's call sign and asked it to pass its message but no reply was heard despite repeated attempts to regain contact. Eastleigh and Bristol continued to call G-AHFV until 12.40hrs without reply. An extensive air and sea search was soon under way but despite reports of flotsam and oil slicks that were reported from aircraft flying in the area the launches were unable to locate anything. The next day pieces of wreckage were salvaged from Freshwater Bay, which bore positive identification markings from the lost aircraft.

On 8 July 1947, the bodies of the two unfortunate crewmen were washed ashore at Brook. The pilot had been twenty-four-year-old Capt. W.A. Shepherd, an experienced RAF pilot who had joined Air Transport Association Ltd only five weeks prior to the accident and although endorsed to fly Ansons had little experience on the type. His radio officer had been Mr K.M. Prim, who at thirty-two years old was an experienced service trained operator. The post-mortem report concluded both had died instantaneously as a result of massive injuries and not due to drowning. The enquiry into the crash found it impossible to positively determine the cause of the crash owing to insufficient evidence but concluded that the circumstances suggested that it was the result of the pilot flying into the sea or losing control whilst in sea fog. Engine failure due to fuel starvation may also have been a contributory factor.

At the end of 1947 two aircraft crashed on consecutive days with fatal results in both instances. On 19 November Short S.25 G-AGHW flew into Brighstone Down killing the First Officer and badly injuring the rest of the crew. The aircraft had been manufactured by Shorts as a Sunderland, and as serial ML725 had been issued to Transport Command before passing to British Overseas Aircraft Corporation (BOAC) on 27 August 1943 for conversion to civilian use as a Short Hythe class aircraft and had been named 'Hamilton'. At the time of the accident the aircraft was on a positioning flight from Hythe to Poole from where later in the day it was due to embark on a scheduled flight to the Far East. The aircraft took off from Southampton Water at 08.00hrs that morning into a 10/10ths cloud base down to 450ft with visibility between 3,000-3,500yds. Immediately the machine was airborne, the radio Officer contacted Southampton control with the standard departure and destination signal and asked if he should change frequency to Poole control. Southampton was busy with another aircraft and requested G-AGHW to wait. At 08.04hrs the signal was repeated to Poole who acknowledged at 08.05hrs. From 08.20hrs both radio stations repeatedly called the flying boat to no avail. G-AGHW had ploughed into the 165-metre high Brighstone Down at 08.12hrs at a spot known as Gallibury Fields.

At the inquiry, the pilot stated that after take off he had climbed to 200ft and commenced a gentle climbing turn to port onto a course of 200 degrees magnetic, the aircraft entering cloud at about 300ft continued to climb up to 1,000ft. by which time the aircraft was flying in and out of cloud layers. At this point, the Pilot synchronised his two compasses, rechecking them a few minutes later. He informed his First Officer that he intended to fly along the coast and asked him to look out for it. After six or seven minutes the First Officer pointed out a river he had spotted through a gap in the clouds. The Captain without reference to his maps presumed this to be the Lymington River as it was on their intended track. Their course was therefore maintained on the basis of this error and two minutes later a small break in the cloud revealed a glimpse of the sea below. The Captain continued on his heading until he estimated he would be clear of the western tip of the Island and then altered course to between 260-270 degrees magnetic and started to descend expecting to break cloud cover well to the west of the Island and fly 'contact' over the sea following the coast line from a point west of Hurst Castle all the way to Poole.

After the machine had been descending through cloud for about two minutes, the First Officer shouted that he could see the ground through the mist. Visibility was almost nil and the pilot immediately pulled hard back on the control column but was too late to prevent an impact with the hillside. The Captain noted that at the time of the First officer's warning the altimeter was reading 500ft. Four people working near the crash site heard the aircraft pass overhead but due to the visibility being less than 20ft could not see it. A few seconds later they heard the engines stop abruptly followed by two loud thuds and realising that it had crashed they raced approximately half a mile to the scene to render what assistance they could. Upon finding the site, they discovered a trail of wreckage strewn up the line of the hillside with a large fire burning in the middle of the scene and several smaller fires within other parts of the carnage. The aircraft had initially struck some way below the summit of the hill losing its starboard wing whilst the fuselage careered on up the slope uprooting trees before finally coming to rest upside down 200 yards further on. Before their arrival the Engineer, Mr E.F. Boncey (who incidentally had been a regular player for

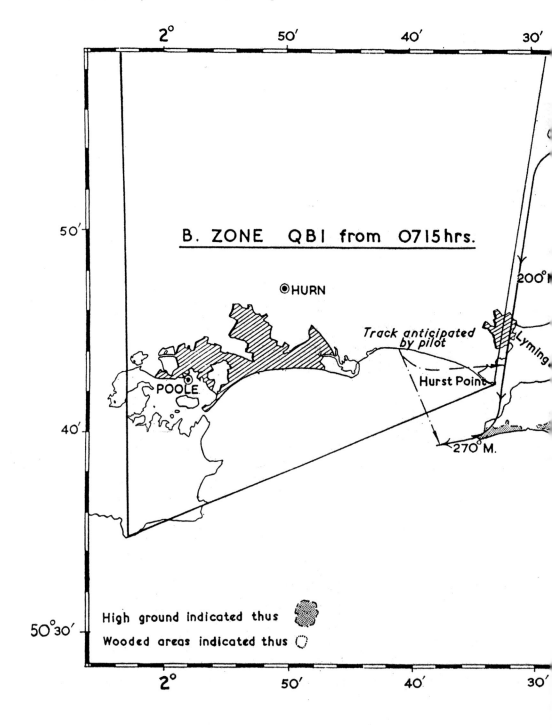

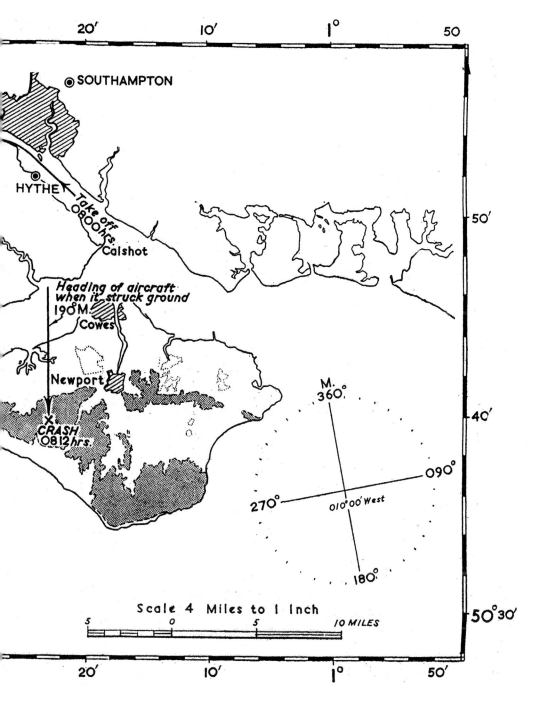

20' 10' |° 50

⊙ SOUTHAMPTON

HYTHE

Take off
0800hrs.

Calshot

Heading of aircraft
when it struck ground
190°M.
Cowes

Newport

X
CRASH
0812hrs.

50'

40'

M.
360°

090°

270°
010°00'West

180°

Scale 4 Miles to 1 inch

5   0   5   10 MILES

50°30'

20' 10' |° 50'

Newport Football Club the year before); had extricated himself and with the help of the Pilot, Captain F.H. Perkins, had rescued the severely injured Radio Officer, Mr G.M. Galer. The unfortunate First Officer, Mr G.K. Whitefoot, had been killed instantly. The Engineer, despite a deep gash to his forehead, set off to find help and followed a track for nearly two miles before coming across some cottages from where he was taken by car to the nearest phone. The police and ambulance were summoned and duly arrived near the scene at 09.20hrs, the ambulance being unable to cover the rough terrain its contents were transferred to a tractor and trailer. In the meantime the four local witnesses had worked brilliantly, extricating the body of the First officer from the wreckage, rendering first aid to the two crew that had remained on site as well as putting out most of the fires amongst the wreckage.

The official accident report on the incident stated that the aircraft was well maintained with all equipment in working order having been completely refurbished and a new certificate of airworthiness issued only four months before the accident. At the time of the crash the aircraft's total time in the air amounted to 6,189 hours. The Pilot and First Officer were ex-service personnel with considerable experience both of general flying and of Sunderland flying.

The crash investigators stated in their conclusions that:

> It is not possible to reconcile either the aircraft's heading at the time it struck the ground or the position of the crash with the courses given by the pilot. At the time of the crash, the visibility was about 20yds and in consequence there was insufficient time for the pilot to have altered course after the ground was seen.
> The evidence suggests that the pilot had intended turning onto a course of 270 deg. M during the descent but that he had not yet done so. A possible explanation of the discrepancy may be that his recollections of the events immediately prior to the crash are confused as a result of his injuries.

The opinion of the investigators was that the accident was the result of flying into high ground in conditions of low cloud and poor visibility. This must be attributed to navigational errors by the pilot.

The following day Avro Anson G-AIWW flew into one of the wartime radar pylons on St Boniface Down at Ventnor killing its two crewmembers. The Anson, service serial MG569, had been purchased from the Air Ministry in November 1946 by its present operators, British Air Transport Ltd, and completely overhauled and converted for freight carrying with a new Certificate of Airworthiness (C of A) being issued in October. Following the issue of the C of A, further radio and system checks were carried out before the machine entered service, making its first working flight on 16 November. On the 20th G-AIWW had taken off from Croydon airport on only its fourth regular newspaper freight service flight to the Channel Islands just after 06.00hrs, the Captain having filed a flight plan showing that he planned to fly at 1,500ft. under instrument flight rules at a true air speed of 135mph and that his 'point of first intended landing' was Jersey. The aircraft would be in radio contact with ground stations throughout the flight. At 06.50hrs the aircraft, some fifteen miles west of its

Aproximate track of aircraft G-AIWW with estimated positions shown

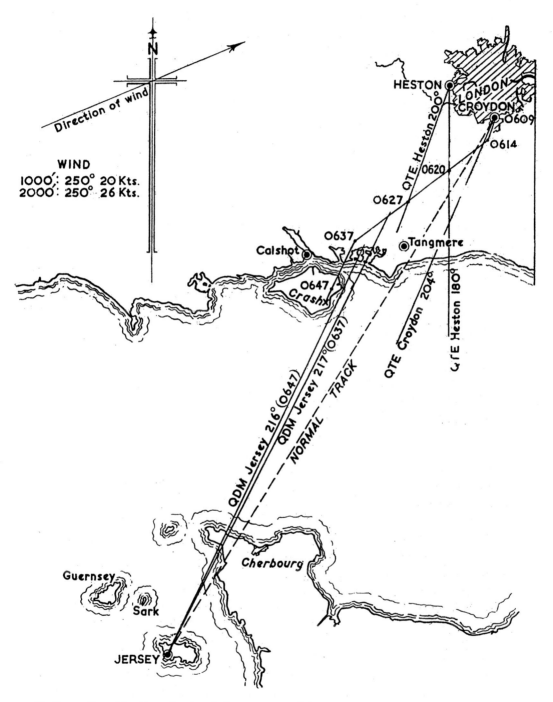

© *Crown Copyright. Reproduced with the permission of the controller of HMSO and the Queen's Printer for Scotland.*

intended course, flying at around 900ft. above sea level struck one of the 240ft high radar towers approximately half way up shattering the starboard wing with the main body of wreckage coming to rest some 350yds further on. One of the four uprights of the pylon and some its internal structure had been shattered but the pylon remained upright and the red beacon at its summit remained lit. Following the impact the remains of aircraft had nose dived into the ground and had disintegrated with the violence of the crash but had not caught fire. Such was the severity of the damage there had been no chance of survival for the crew which had comprised of E.G. Snowden (pilot) and R.J. Corrie (radio officer), who were both ex service personnel.

Once again the weather had been a major factor in the loss of an aircraft. The conditions were similar to those of the previous days crash with visibility at St Catherine's Point officially recorded as 2,200yds and 10/10ths cloud down to 700ft, whilst local witnesses at St Boniface stated that the Down was completely shrouded in mist with visibility down to only a few yards.

The Anson had asked for and received several bearing plots from the ground stations at Croydon and Uxbridge, the first of the Uxbridge plots at 06.20hrs. showed the Anson to be west of its intended track whilst a second plot at 06.27hrs showed it still farther west of track. At 06.29hrs the pilot informed Uxbridge that he was over the coast, although in fact he was still a considerable way inland. It may be that in the dawn light and low cloud conditions that existed in the area the pilot may have mistaken some land feature for the coast, or more probably that he had sent the message 'over coast' on his estimated time of arrival over the coast on the assumption that he was on track. His normal track would have seen him over fly the coast near Tangmere in Sussex whilst in fact he actually crossed the coast over Portsmouth.

Captain Snowden had received a favourable weather report for Jersey and it is believed that thinking he had cleared the coast at 06.29hrs he could safely begin a descent from around 1,500ft to fly on to his destination below the cloud level.

The accident enquiry board findings were that the aircraft was well within weight limits and was well maintained and that the engines were functioning at the moment of the crash. There had been no pre-crash failure of the aircraft or of any of its systems and that all information requested from ground radio stations had been efficiently transmitted to the aircraft and had been noted in the radio officer's log book. It concluded that the accident was the result of flying into an obstacle on high ground in conditions of low cloud and poor visibility; and that this must be attributed to an error of navigation on the part of the pilot.

At 11.50hrs on 6 June 1949 Cowes Police telephoned the Air Accidents Investigation Branch of the CAA to report a crash. Ninety minutes earlier a de Havilland D.H 98A (Rapide) had crashed near the south-west boundary of Somerton Airfield. The Rapide, civil registration G-AGPI, had been on a scheduled flight from Southampton and attempted its landing onto the SSW runway at Somerton and after running along the runway for some distance took off again but failed to gain height and struck a tree just outside the airfield perimeter and crashed into the field beyond. The Rapide's pilot, Captain (Civilian rank) Selwyn Richardson DFC, DFM, was seriously injured and six of the eight passengers on board suffered injuries.

De Havilland DH98A, Dragon Rapide. (Air Britain)

The aircraft had been converted from an RAF de Havilland Dominie trainer (NR809) in 1945 and had been overhauled and a new certificate of airworthiness issued as recently as November 1948 and immediately prior to the crash was considered to be in good condition. Twenty-six-year-old Richardson had achieved the rank of Flight Lieutenant during his RAF service and had amassed some 1,250 hours of service flying before his demob in 1946, when he took up a civil licence and added a further 1,440 hours of which 800 were in Rapides. He had joined Somerton Airways in April 1949 and had successfully landed at Somerton on over eighty occasions.

The weather conditions on the morning of the crash were favourable; with a 9 knot easterly wind and $\frac{6}{8}$ Cumulus cloud at 2,500ft and eight miles visibility. Earlier that morning Richardson had already landed at Cowes carrying passengers from Portsmouth. On this flight he had used the NE runway but had stated that because this runway sloped downhill and had a rough surface he would use the SSW runway on his next flight because it was uphill and had a less obstructed approach path.

The aircraft departed Southampton (Eastleigh) at 10.11hrs carrying eight passengers, two of whom were non fare paying children, and in order to make more room for the passengers Richardson had opted to leave his Radio Operator behind at Southampton.

Witnesses reported that when the aircraft arrived at Somerton airfield it proceeded to make a rather high and fast approach to the SSW runway touching down between a third and half-way along its 700-yard length and running for approximately 200yds.

The machine maintained a high speed during this run and the pilot, fearing he would over-run the runway, opened up the throttles and attempted to go around again. With rising ground and only 200yds of runway left, the Rapide failed to gain enough height to clear a 25ft poplar tree just outside the airfield perimeter. The starboard wing was extensively damaged and further damage was caused to the airframe as the machine struck the chimney pots of a nearby bungalow before crashing into the ground 120yds from the airfield. The final impact was severe and the starboard wing and cockpit area were completely shattered.

Captain Richardson told the accident enquiry that he was puzzled by the speed at which the aircraft travelled along the ground after touchdown and that apart from the fact that the engines seemed slow to respond to the re-opening of the throttle he had no explanation to offer as to why the aircraft failed to clear the tree.

Examination of the wreckage found no pre-crash defects but did discover that several of the passenger's seats had broken away from their fixing brackets in the crash. They were removed and sent for laboratory examination which subsequently reported that: 'Examination of the fittings revealed that the amount of welding connecting the strap to the floor plate was inadequate, attachment being by a 'lick' of weld only 2 or 3 hundredths of an inch thick. The weld metal had been applied without heating the floor plate sufficiently so that cold weld metal was deposited without fusion'. These fittings were not manufactured by de Havilland.

The observations of the enquiry were that the fast approach of the aircraft, its long float before touchdown and its high speed on the ground could be accounted for by the tail wind when landing in a SSW direction. This would also have had an adverse effect on the subsequent take off attempt and would explain the failure to gain height. The enquiry laid the blame squarely on the pilot who they concluded misjudged his approach and did not take overshoot action until it was too late.

On 28 January 1953, at approximately 02.00hrs, Short S25 Sunderland III G-AGKY's take off run down the Solent came to an abrupt end $1\frac{3}{4}$ nautical miles north-east of Cowes between Hill Head and Prince Consort Buoys. The accident occurred as the aircraft attempted to take off on the first leg of a scheduled service flight to Madeira via Lisbon. The Captain of the Aquilla Airlines flying boat, Mr J.W. Jessop, found that he was unable to maintain a straight course and he aborted the take off about half way along the flare path. As he throttled back the four Pegasus engines the port wing dipped violently forcing its tip mounted float into the sea and causing damage to the float. The aircraft swung sharply to port, submerging its port wing up to the outer engine. This was inspite of the valiant attempts of the flight crew, who after scrabbling out of the 'astro-dome' hatch on the upper fuselage made their way in the dark and wet conditions to the opposite wing tip in an attempt to balance the aircraft. Their combined weight was insufficient to level the aircraft and the Captain stopped the engines and weathercocked the stricken airliner into the wind.

Captain Jessop radioed for the company launch at the upwind end of the flare path to come alongside and 'clear ship'. This was carried out in orderly fashion and the twenty-six passengers were disembarked in around ten minutes; including four passengers who had followed the crew through the astro-dome onto the fuselage top

Short Flying Boat, capsized off Calshot Spit. This is almost certainly G-AGKY. (C. Dover)

and who had to be safely recovered back into the hull. The passengers were taken initially to Calshot before being transferred to Southampton. All of the luggage, freight, and mail that G-AGKY was carrying were off loaded next. Before the machine was taken in tow by a rescue launch from RAF Calshot the petrol in its port wing tanks was jettisoned in an attempt to level the wings. The tow back to Calshot went without incident but as the aircraft was being positioned for mooring the list to port suddenly increased and the Sunderland heeled over and sank.

The flying boat had been in good condition before the incident, having flown some 8,840 hours since being built in 1944 by Short Brothers. It had originally been on strength with RAF Transport Command as ML789 before being transferred to BOAC on 28 July 1944 where it was given the name *Hungerford*. It was transferred to Aquilla Airways in January 1949.

The subsequent enquiry into the crash laid the blame mainly on the Captain but with contributory factors apportioned on the control officer who had laid out the flare path and to a sudden deterioration in the weather.

Unlike a conventional land based aircraft which uses runways which are fixed, a seaplane's take-off route is laid out onto the surface of the water according to local conditions based mainly on the prevailing wind direction at the time. It was the responsibility of the control officer, Mr J.H. Grover, to select the take off route,

A close up of G-AGKY beached at Calshot following an accident. Personnel left to right: V. Pitt, J. Flaws, L. Hartford & 'Digger' Seymour. (V. Pitt via N. Hull)

ensure it was clear of floating debris and at night to mark it clearly with green flares positioned dead into wind. The flare path for this take off was approximately 2,000yds long with flares at 500-yard intervals and a launch displaying a green light positioned at each end. Despite having worked for Aquilla since the previous year and having handled around 100 night takeoffs Grover had only performed the flare path laying duty on one previous occasion. At 12.00hrs on 27 July, Grover visited Southampton Met. Office and checked the forecast wind for 00.45hrs on 28 July was west-south-west at 12 knots. At about 23.00hrs he confirmed there was no appreciable change in the forecast and fifty-five minutes later left Southampton in the control pinnacle accompanied by Southampton Harbour Board Control officer who was responsible for safety in regard to shipping in the harbour area. It was agreed to lay the flare path in the area between Hill Head and the Prince Consort Buoys. On arrival at the Hill Head Buoy Grover stopped the pinnacle and estimated the wind direction 'by feeling the wind on his face' and having selected a distant light in West Cowes to gain a bearing on which to steer commenced laying the flares. The laying of the flares commenced about 00.40hrs and was completed by around 01.55hrs. Interrogation of all those involved following the accident indicated that the flare path was laid on a bearing of 210 degrees.

G-AGKY arrived at the take off point at about 01.50hrs and the captain carried out his pre-flight engine and instrument checks and found everything in order. He checked the bearing of the flare path using his radio compass and finding it was 210 degrees, and different to the forecast wind asked the control officer what was the relationship of the wind to the flare path. Grover replied that the wind was 5-10 degrees to starboard of the flare path at 12 knots. In order to counteract the side wind the take off run was started with the starboard aileron in the full up position and with full left rudder applied. Nos 2, 3, & 4 engines were set to full power whilst No.1 engine was running at 1,000rpm. Almost immediately the aircraft started to swing to starboard and the pilot corrected this by throttling No.1 engine still further. As the machine gathered speed he throttled No.1 engine back up to approx. half power and the aircraft started to lift up onto its hull and achieve a planing attitude. They were now travelling at just over 40 knots. when the weather suddenly deteriorated, visibility dropping to around 1,000 yards due to heavy rain. The nose of the aircraft started to rise and fall and a swing to starboard was corrected by throttling back No.1 engine. By this time the aircraft was fast approaching the third flare along its take off run and Captain Jessop decided to abort the take off. As the throttles were closed the flying boat's port wing dipped and the float was damaged. At 01.58hrs the captain instructed radio officer Whitfield to inform the control officer that they had lost the port wing float and to stand by to give assistance.

The enquiry board presented its findings in July of that year. It criticised the Captain for committing an 'error of airmanship by not ascertaining the true crosswind and in consequence attempting to take off under conditions with which he could not contend'. It also blamed the control officer for misinforming the pilot.

The control officer had in fact laid the flare path some 35 degrees out of wind and by the time the take off run commenced this had increased to 50 degrees out of wind.

De Havilland Chipmunk: Basic Trainer.

The Southampton met. Office records showed that at 02.00 hours the wind direction was 260/270 degrees with a speed of 13/15 knots although gusts to 20 knots were recorded at about the time of take off. The wreckage of G-AGKY was salvaged but such was the damage that the aircraft was scrapped in May of that year

Four years later another Aquilla Airways S25 scheduled service on that route took off from Southampton Water. It was soon to suffer a much worse fate

At about 22.46hrs on 15 November 1957, the four-engined Short Solent flying boat G-AKNU, owned by Aquilla Airways Limited, took off from Southampton Water on a scheduled flight to Lisbon, en route for Madeira, with fifty passengers and a crew of eight. It made a normal climb, and, three minutes later, passed a routine departure message to Southern Air Traffic Control Centre – London. At 22.54hrs, however, the Radio Officer called the Aquilla base at Southampton and transmitted this message: 'No.4 engine feathered. Coming back in a hurry.' Approximately one minute later the aircraft crashed into the face of a quarry between Chessel and Brook in the Isle of Wight. The wreckage caught fire and, despite the devoted efforts of a number of people who quickly came to the scene, none of the crew and only fifteen of the passengers survived.

The above is the opening paragraph from the official enquiry report and it coldly and efficiently précis' the events leading up to the Island's worst air crash. This was the second Short Sunderland derivative to crash on the Island and happened almost exactly ten years to the day after the previous Sunderland crash at Brighstone detailed earlier.

The aircraft had begun its career as Short Sunderland serial NJ207 with 201 Sqdn, before being converted to a Solent Mk III by Short & Harland Ltd. She was first registered on 25 July 1948 and passed into the ownership of Aquilla Airways on 15 November 1951, having at that time only amassed a total of 8 hours and 50 minutes flying time. Aquilla Airlines named their aircraft and G-AKNU was originally given the name *Sydney*, later lengthened to *City of Sydney*. At the time of the accident she had flown a total of 5,480 hours, 863 of which had been since her last total overhaul. The enquiry board found that the aircraft's state of maintenance was generally good and that several small defects that had been reported before the flight had apparently been attended to satisfactorily.

The aircraft's tanks contained 2,000 gallons of fuel which along with the wreckage burned fiercely creating flames estimated to have reached 40–50ft high. Despite the relatively remote area of the crash, rescuers were on the scene extremely quickly and comprised local farm workers, and by luck, several soldiers who had been on a night exercise in the immediate area. It was reported at the time that over half of the survivors undoubtedly owed their lives to the selfless heroics of two Army Officers and a senior N.C.O. who repeatedly braved the inferno to drag out injured passengers until, with their own clothes alight, they were finally beaten back by the terrifying heat.

Wreckage of G-AKNU Sydney *following crash at Chessel Down on 15 November 1957. View looking approximately north. (V. Pitt via N. Hull)*

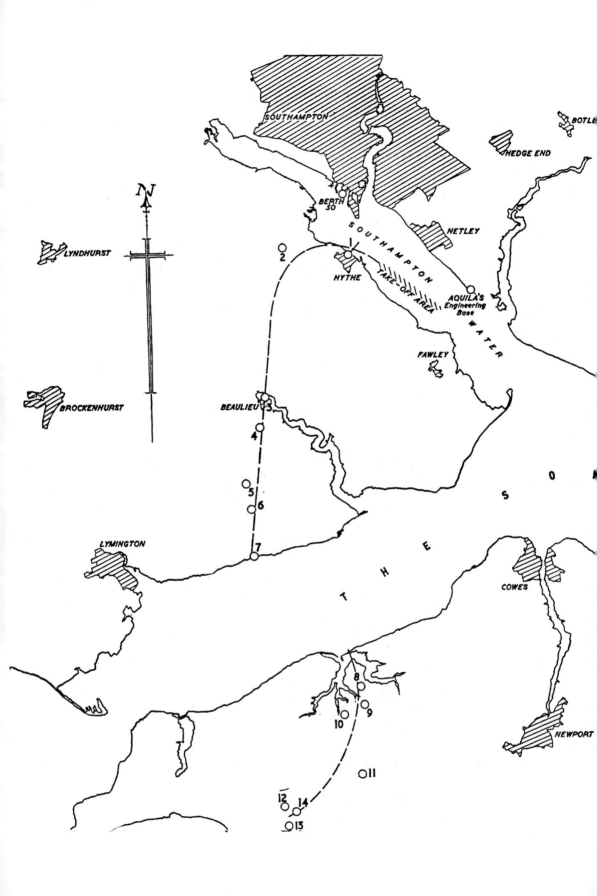

Estimated flight path of G-AKNU on 15 November 1957

 WICKHAM

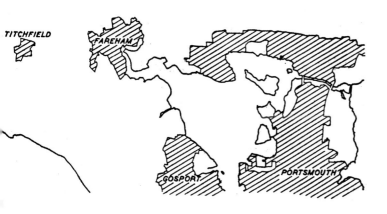

TITCHFIELD

FAREHAM

GOSPORT · PORTSMOUTH

E

N

T

KEY

1. POLICE CONSTABLE GALE
2. MR. BRETT
3. MR. ELSWORTH
4. MRS. HISCOCK
5. MR. WINSEY
6. MR. PHILLIPS
7. MR. MILLER
8. MR. BARTON
9. MR. E.W. POCOCK
   MR. J.W.E. POCOCK
10. MR. DOWNER
11. MR. SIVIER
12. MR. & MRS. JOLLY
13. MAJOR WELLER
    LIEUT. SHERBURN
    C.Q.M.S., REID
14. MR. BRUCE

 STATUTE MILES

NAUTICAL MILES

Chessel Down crash site, taken in 1995, viewed from the south. The Chalk Pit still bears the scars of the 1957 crash. (N. Hull)

By Sunday afternoon, the crash site had become a sightseeing spectacle, thousands of people flocking from all parts of the Island to view the scene of devastation. A large force of police, assisted by special constables and members of several motoring organisations where drafted in to keep the record traffic stream flowing. Sadly that evening the cordon guarding the upper edge of the chalk pit where the wreckage still lay had to apprehend and turn back a number of ghoulish souvenir hunters who attempted to crawl past them in the darkness.

The three soldiers who had featured so prominently in the rescue had been parked barely 200yds from the crash site waiting for the completion of a night exercise involving thirty-six soldiers they had been in charge of. As they sat waiting they first heard the aircraft and then saw it approaching from the direction of Calbourne. Major W.J.F. Weller reported that the engines seem to be running unevenly and he estimated the aircraft's height to be no more than 100ft. All the cabin lights and navigation lights were clearly visible and with its forward landing lights illuminating the top of the quarry the aircraft banked abruptly to starboard and crashed headlong into the slope of the chalk face.

Major Weller sent his driver to telephone for help and ran with his two colleagues, Lt Sherburn and QMS Ried, towards the inferno. On arrival at the crash site they found that the tail section was not yet on fire, and amazingly two women were walking, apparently unharmed, away from it. Seven other passengers were lying badly burned on the ground near to the wreckage. The three soldiers proceeded into the wreckage dragging other injured, some with their fuel soaked clothes alight, and the dead from the carnage. Q.M.S Ried, who lost his moustache in the rescue attempts, praised the Major who with his own shirt alight had been the last rescuer to leave the burning wreckage.

The occupant of Chessel farm had been in her bedroom when she heard the aircraft approaching. It was so loud that she feared it was about to hit the farmhouse and as she stared from the window to try and locate the machine it hurtled past scant feet from her roof top with its occupants clearly visible in the glow from the cabin lights.

The most seriously injured were transferred in a fleet of private cars to St Mary's hospital where a complete ward had rapidly been vacated to make room for them. The walking wounded were taken to Fairlee Hospital where one survivor, a Mr Mangham described the brief flight as 'worse than a ride on Blackpool's Big Dipper.' He went on to relate how they were late starting their flight, the pilot revving and then cutting the engines several times until after thirty minutes of taxiing the flying boat finally took off. A few moments after take off the plane dropped then climbed before dropping again. This went on for about five minutes before a white faced Steward came back from the flight deck and gave the passengers a thumbs up before announcing, 'Things are a bit sticky'. As he returned to the flight deck the plane dropped once more. There was a grinding noise then everything went black. Mr Mangham then sensed smoke and smelt burning, his wife told him to kick the window out and after a couple of attempts he managed to do so and jumped blindly out into the darkness closely followed by his wife and two other passengers.

During the night the first seventeen bodies were recovered and removed to a makeshift mortuary set up in the rifle range at Albany Barracks. Back at the crash site conditions were becoming more difficult for the rescue teams. By 04.00hrs the fires were out but the metalwork was still red hot and the thousands of gallons of water and fire fighting foam that had been used to extinguish the flames had turned the site into a slippery quagmire. Rescue work was abandoned until dawn when firemen and soldiers resumed the grim task of recovering the last bodies of the forty-three who had perished. These last remains proved the most difficult to reach, being trapped under the engines of the aircraft which had fallen to the ground as the wreckage disintegrated. The engines having to be dragged clear by teams of men using ropes, which frequently broke under the incredible strain.

Even before the last of the bodies had been found, accident inspectors had arrived to begin their meticulous task of finding the cause of the tragic incident. Their conclusions were that the aircraft had flown into high ground, the impact point being 300ft above sea level, whilst flying on only its two port engines. The starboard outer-engine's propeller was fully 'feathered' whilst the inner engine's was not and would have been windmilling; the fuel actuators for both starboard engines were set to the 'stop' position. The aircraft's speed at the moment of impact was close to, if not at, its stalling point.

The cause of the crash was quite clearly that both starboard engines had stopped. The craft could have returned quite safely to Southampton water on three engines. Why they stopped was never discovered, there were no defects subsequently found in the engines themselves, the conclusion being that the aircraft crashed due to the stoppage of the No.3 engine at a time when the No.4 engine was also stopped. Why No.4 stopped is unknown whilst the cause of the stoppage to No.3 was either an electrical failure in the fuel cut off circuit or the accidental operation of the cut-off switch.

The enquiry was at pains to point out that the pilot, Capt. F.W. Eltis, should not be criticised for his handling of the aircraft – the fact that he managed to control it for so long was a measure of his gallant attempt to nurse his disabled plane to a place of safety. As a consequence of this crash guards were fitted over the fuel actuators on other Aquilla Airway's Solents to prevent accidental operation.

The longer-term effects of the crash of a 35-ton aircraft were reported in the *Isle of Wight County Press* some six months later. The 19 April 1958 edition carried a report that the pollution of the water supply caused by the disaster continued to be a problem for the Water Board. A Water Board engineer told the *Isle of Wight County Press* that, on the previous Monday the affected supply had been reinstated but that

Douglas Dakota (DC3) G-AGZB which crashed on 6 May 1962 at St Boniface Down, Ventnor. (Air Britain)

over the next two days complaints about the water quality had been received from the Shalfleet, Thorley and Ningwood areas and that the supply had once again been shut off. The Water Board engineer explained that the only way of clearing the oil from the water supply was by pumping it to waste, and that so far over one million gallons had been lost in this way.

6 May 1962 brought another airliner tragedy when Dakota G-AGZB flew into the summit of St Boniface Down. The twin-engined aircraft had been manufactured as a C-47 transport in 1943 by Douglas Aircraft Inc. in Santa Monica. It had carried the military serial FZ624 before being first registered as a British civil aircraft in 1946 for British European Airways, passing into the ownership of East Anglian Flying Services Ltd (Channel Airways) in December 1960.

On the day of the accident the machine had been on a scheduled flight from Jersey to Portsmouth and on to Southend and had departed Jersey at 13.54hrs. The weather conditions had been bad for the previous two days and the passengers, all of whom were booked to Portsmouth, had been informed that weather conditions were bad at Portsmouth and if they could not land they would be flying on to Southend. At 14.07hrs G-AGZB reported to Jersey that Alderney was in sight and they were flying at 3,000ft, seven minutes later they radioed that they were at the FIR boundary and were changing radio frequency to that of London FIR. Up to this point the weather appears to have been clear. One minute later Zulu Bravo called London FIR requesting permission to let down to 1,000ft, London replied that there was no known traffic and the new flight level would be permitted. Zulu Bravo acknowledged and requested confirmation of the local QNH*, which was transmitted to them. The repeated confirmation of the reading transmitted back from the aircraft was the last transmission received from Zulu Bravo.

At 14.28 hours, through the low cloud and drizzle at Woody Point, just west of Ventnor, the local coastguard logged the passing of a low flying aircraft; a little later an aircraft was seen flying low over Ventnor Railway station towards St Boniface Down which was enveloped in cloud. Shortly afterwards came the sound of a crash on the upper slopes of the down. Inspection of the crash site revealed that the aircraft had initially struck the side of the down at a height of 717ft above sea level. It bounced onwards through a high perimeter fence surrounding the disused RAF radar site, coming to rest 840ft forward and 74ft higher up the slope from the initial point of contact, which itself was scarcely 1,000yds from Ventnor town centre. The machine caught fire on impact. A Wroxall farmworker who had working in the immediate area ran to the scene and managed to drag the stewardess and another passenger from the burning wreck and rendering first aid to other survivors before setting out to summon help.

The crash immediately claimed the lives of the pilot, Capt. P.M. de Diesbach; First Officer, Mr E.Y. Fitzakerly; the stewardess, Miss P. Groves, who had been heroically dragged from the wreckage died in hospital from her injuries. Of the fourteen passengers aboard, eight perished at the scene with one further fatally injured, the remaining five received serious injuries.

Accident to Dakota G–AGZB. 6 May 1962

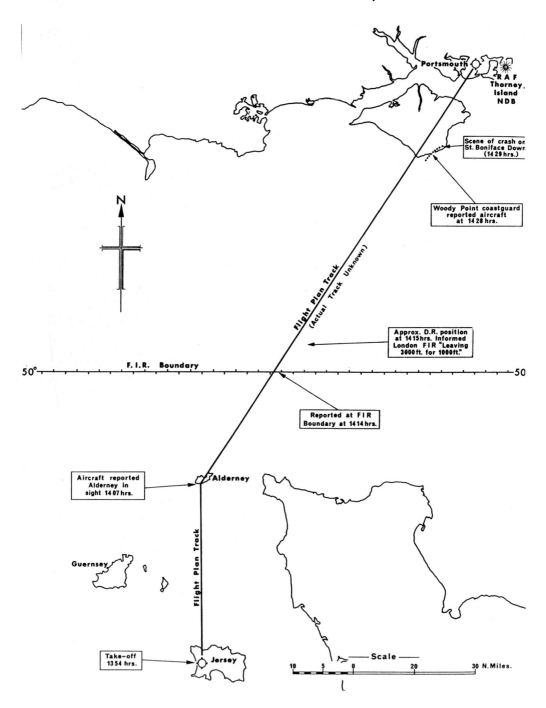

Portsmouth

RAF
Thorney.
Island
NDB

Scene of crash on
St. Boniface Down
(14 29 hrs.)

Woody Point coastguard
reported aircraft
at 14 28 hrs.

N

Flight Plan Track
(Actual Track Unknown)

Approx. D.R. position
at 14 15hrs. Informed
London FIR "Leaving
3000ft. for 1000ft."

F.I.R. Boundary

50°

50

Reported at FIR
Boundary at 14 14 hrs.

Aircraft reported
Alderney in
sight 14 07 hrs.

Alderney

Guernsey

Flight Plan Track

Take-off
13 54 hrs.

Jersey

Scale

10   5   0   20   30 N.Miles.

US Army crash recovery vessel undertaking the sombre task of recovering the Catalina Flying Boat from Southampton water on 27 July 1998. (Southern Daily Echo)

The official report into the crash found that at the time of impact, both engines were developing power, and that both the undercarriage and flaps had been in the flight position. There was no evidence of pre-crash failure or malfunction in any of the aircraft's equipment. Both altimeters were recovered from the crash site and, although badly damaged, were found to be set to the correct QNH setting. Portsmouth Airport had no radio communication or radio direction finding equipment and the flight would have been relying on the Non Directional Beacon (NDB) at nearby RAF Thorney Island for its bearings; although no specific instructions on the use of this NDB were included in the company's operations manual.

The opinion of the enquiry board was that the accident occurred because as a result of an error of airmanship the aircraft was flown below a safe altitude in bad weather conditions and struck cloud covered ground. It made a recommendation that scheduled passenger services should only operate into airports with radio communication facilities.

The early evening television news on 27 July 1998 carried a dramatic report on another local aviation tragedy. At 13.44 hours that afternoon a Super Catalina amphibious aircraft operated by Duxford-based Plain Sailing Ltd had been attempting its second touch and go approach over Southampton water when things went horribly wrong.

The 1944-built aircraft had been on a promotion visit to launch a proposed seaplane event known as 'Seawings 2000'. The aircraft operator had offered some flights free of charge to the organisers. The fourteen passenger seats had been allocated to the Press, members of Southampton City Council, various other VIPs with the remaining seats going to people involved in assisting with the event. In addition, the Catalina carried a crew of four.

The twin-engined amphibian had taken off at around 13.30hrs from Southampton Airport and had flown down the River Itchen to a point on Southampton Water between Netley and Hythe. The pilot completed the 'pre-landing (water) checklist', part of which requires the pilot to confirm that the floats are extended, landing gear retracted and the nose gear doors closed. With the checklist successfully completed the pilot carried out a left-hand circuit approach and the aircraft was let down onto the water, lightly skimming the surface during its short run before taking off again.

A second touch and go landing was then attempted. A photo taken of the machine as it passed Hythe Marina appeared to show the aircraft correctly configured for a water landing. The crew reported that the touchdown was normal. After a few seconds the pilot noticed the wake of a boat ahead and called to the co-pilot to increase the engine power. The co-pilot reckoned he had increased the throttle settings to about half power by the time they crossed the wake. A cabin crewmember that was sat in the front passenger cabin saw a fierce jet of water erupt from the bottom of the cockpit bulkhead and almost immediately the aircraft swerved viciously to port. As soon as the craft had come to rest and with the fuselage rapidly filling with water the crew started to evacuate the two passenger cabins.

The Catalina settled into a semi-submerged position with its wing upper surfaces above water level and its nose on the river bottom. The co-pilot had scrambled out onto the upper wing surface and with the pilot tried to carry out a head count. This was difficult because several small boats had already arrived on scene and had started to pick survivors from the water. It soon became apparent that at least one passenger from the forward cabin was unaccounted for. By now, the aircraft had settled further and the fuselage was almost completely submerged. The pilot bravely attempted to dive down to the forward escape hatch but was unsuccessful and was eventually persuaded to give up and allow himself to be rescued. Meanwhile the co-pilot had been attempting to search the rear cabin.

The bedraggled survivors were taken to hospital where examination showed that their injuries were minor, consisting of bruising and minor cuts. Coastguard divers later recovered the bodies of two passengers; Mr M. Andrews (Mayor of Southampton) and airport worker Mr P. Shave from the forward cabin. It would seem that these two passengers stayed behind in the cabin to assist others to escape.

By just after 16.00hrs that afternoon the aircraft was stabilised and then raised clear

Blackburn Rippon, S1569, following forced-landing. This is believed to be in Howgate Road, Bembridge. (Via P. Newberry)

of the water by the US Army salvage vessel *Pine Lodge* which had been mobilised within minutes of the crash from its Marchwood base. The recovered aircraft had suffered very little damage. Most damage to the airframe apparently caused by the lifting strops used during the salvage operation. However, both nose landing gear doors were missing. They had been torn away during the touch and go landing and the resultant water pressure that occurred almost instantly in the wheel bay had breached the forward bulkhead. On examination, it was found that the hydraulic actuating tubes for the wheel bay doors had severe internal corrosion. There was no routine maintenance procedure required for checking the internal surfaces of these tubes. It was considered most likely by the Board of Enquiry that failure of the doors was caused by the corrosion in the actuating arms, although as the doors themselves were never recovered the possibility that they had encountered a substantial piece of flotsam could not be discounted.

The last section of this chapter deals with incidents which have been related to the author but which despite extensive research have not been substantiated or cross referenced with other sources. The first of these 'rumour mill' incidents relayed to me was the forced landing of a Blackburn Rippon, serial S1559 (see photo). The photo clearly shows the aircraft on its nose in a garden, reputedly at Howgate Road, Bembridge. S1559 was a Fleet Air Arm machine and its service history shows that it was built as a Ripon and served as such between 1931 and 1934. It was then recalled to Blackburn's and converted to a Baffin in which form it served mainly in the Mediterranean area. So, it is probable that this incident occurred during the earlier part of its service life.

The next reputed incident occurred not far from that of the Rippon. This was relayed to me as a large single engined machine in the Nunwell area during the late 1940s or early 1950s. The aircraft apparently carrying 'invasion stripe' markings on its wings was described to me as a Republic Thunderbolt or Sea Fury. It would seem unlikely that a Thunderbolt Squadron would be operating in this area; perhaps this incident was actually the Firefly that landed at Sandown marshes or the Harvard incident at Yaverland.

Another incident was the recollection of a forced landing onto Ryde Airport site (now Tesco's) of a troop-carrying glider around the period of the D-Day landings, no further details of this event have come to light. This perhaps would not be surprising, hundreds of gliders were produced for the forthcoming invasion of the European fortress and all of them would be considered as 'one flight aircraft', the extensive records which followed other types of service aircraft would not have been so relevant therefore making it difficult to research.

An intriguing incident mentioned very briefly in a short history of Somerton Airfield was the landing of an undamaged Messerschmitt 109, its pilot mistakenly thinking he was alighting onto one of the Nazi-occupied Channel Islands. Whilst similar events happened on more than one occasion around the country during the war no other source mentions what would have been quite a coup for the Island and surely would have been reported extensively (by wartime standards).

The report of the war time crash near to the centre of the Island of an American

P–51 Mustang piloted by a test pilot is another event that seems not to have generated too much official interest, whilst a similar aircraft's emergency landing at Somerton following extensive battle damage has only come to light in the Somerton History mentioned previously.

The *Christchurch Times* for Saturday 15 August carried a front-page article, which detailed how on the 8th of that month five young Home Guardsmen had attacked a low flying Heinkel He 111 with their Lewis gun scoring several hits. The gun crew had been stationed on the roof of the factory where at least one of them worked (Air Defence Research Establishment at Christchurch) and as the aircraft passed over the factory after bombing in the New Milton area the eighteen-year-old gunners let fly at it. They had tracer ammunition in their Lewis gun so could quite clearly see the effect they were having on the lone bomber. Photocopies of two other documents that were shown to me indicate that the crew of this aircraft baled out in the vicinity of the Island, although research has not turned up a Heinkel loss in the area for this date.

Post-war crashes are generally better reported, as the natural wartime need for secrecy does not apply, and so it is particularly galling that the next incident cannot be traced. No exact dates were given so extensive trawling of local papers' archives and aircraft type records is the only hope for confirmation. So far this has been without success. The report is from an eye witnesses recollection and was related to me as the force-landing into a field near to the railway line just to the Wooton side of Havenstreet Railway Station of a de Havilland Vampire. This was described to me by the fireman of the Newport to Ryde train who stated that the aircraft was down on the left-hand side of the track looking towards Ashey and was so close that as the train passed he was looking down onto it. He said that he does not recollect any report in the press at the time of the crash, around 1960, nor had he heard anything about it since. Certainly no British Vampires have ever crashed in this area. Perhaps it was another type of jet and the witness's identification was a little rusty or maybe it was a foreign aircraft. Further leads or information on any of these would be welcomed, as would comments on any other incidents that have slipped through the net.

Endnote

★ QNH is the 'Q code' abbreviation for local barometric pressure essential for accurate setting of the altimeter.

Appendix 1

Luftwaffe: Command Chain and Unit Designations

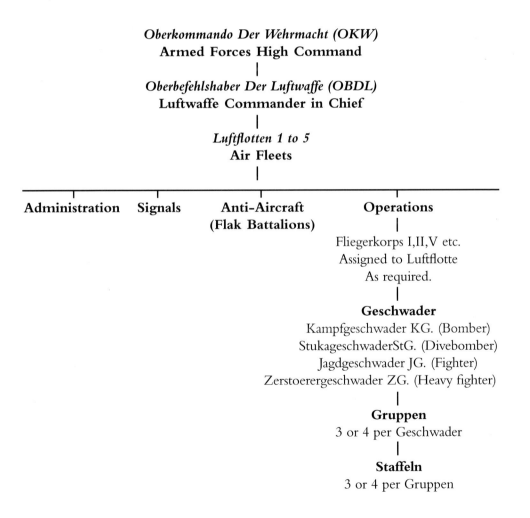

Oberkommando Der Wehrmacht (OKW)
Armed Forces High Command
|
Oberbefehlshaber Der Luftwaffe (OBDL)
Luftwaffe Commander in Chief
|
Luftflotten 1 to 5
Air Fleets
|

Administration   **Signals**   **Anti-Aircraft**   **Operations**
(Flak Battalions) |
Fliegerkorps I,II,V etc.
Assigned to Luftflotte
As required.
|
Geschwader
Kampfgeschwader KG. (Bomber)
StukageschwaderStG. (Divebomber)
Jagdgeschwader JG. (Fighter)
Zerstoerergeschwader ZG. (Heavy fighter)
|
Gruppen
3 or 4 per Geschwader
|
Staffeln
3 or 4 per Gruppen

During the period 1939-1945:
A Luftwaffe Geschwader was roughly equivalent to an RAF Group
A Gruppe was roughly equivalent to a Wing
A Staffel was roughly equivalent to a Squadron.

A Geschwader carried a prefix to denote its function thus:
Erprobungs (Test flight)
Fernaufklarungs (Long range reconnaissance)
Jagd (Day fighter)
Kampf (Bomber)
Nachtjagd (Night-fighter)
Nahaufklarungs (Close reconnaissance)
Schlacht (Close support)
Zerstörer (Heavy fighter)
Geschwader were referred to by abbreviations, e.g. JG = Jagdgeschwader. Gruppe within a Geschwader by a Roman numeral, e.g. I/JG and Staffel by an Arabic numeral, e.g. I/JG 4.

Appendix 2

Comparison of RAF & Luftwaffe Rank Equivalents

(With abbreviations as used throughout text)

Air Chief Marshal	Generalfeldmarschall or Generaloberst
Air Marshal	General der Flieger
Air Vice Marshal	Generalleutnant
Air Commodore	Generalmajor
Group Captain	Oberst (Obst)
Wing Commander (Wg Cdr)	Oberstleutnant (Obltn)
Squadron Leader (Sqdn Ldr)	Major (Maj)
Flight Lieutenant (Flt Lt)	Hauptmann (Hptm)
Flying Officer (Flg-Off)	Oberleutnant (Obltn)
Pilot Officer (P/O)	Leutnant (Lt)
Warrant Officer (W/O)	Stabsfeldwebel (Sfw)
Flight Sergeant (Flt Sgt)	Oberfeldwebel (Obfw)
Sergeant (Sgt)	Feldwebel (F/W)
Corporal (Cpl)	Unteroffizier (Uffz)
Aircraftsman 1st class (A/Cm)	Gefreiter (Gfr)
Aircraftsman 2nd class (A/Cm)	Flieger (Flgr)
No equivalent rank	Sunderführer (Sdfhr)

The title of Kommodore was also used by the Luftwaffe; however this was not an actual rank, rather a designation of 'Unit Leader'.

Appendix 3

Aircraft Damage Repair Categories

Throughout the book, reference is made to aircraft being categorised as Cat. 'C' or similar. Repair categories (Cat.) are used to specify the amount of damage, whether or not the not the aircraft will be repairable and by whom (service unit or return to civilian contractor) and in terminal classes the final fate of the machine.

The category system has changed from time to time to reflect Service requirements and differs between the RAF & Fleet Air Arm.

Pre 1941: RAF & FAA (until May 1939 all FAA aircraft were on charge to the RAF).

U   Undamaged
M(u) Repairable on site by unit
M(c) Beyond repair on site
R(B) Dismantle for return to factory
W   Written off

1941-1952: RAF
U   Undamaged
A   Repairable on site by unit
AC Repair beyond on site unit
B   Beyond repair on site
C   To use as ground instructional airframe
E   Write off (sub categories of E below)
E.1 Reduce to components for selective re-use
E.2 Scrap
E.3 Burnt out
Em Missing

1952-1961: RAF

T1	Undamaged
Cat.2	Repairable by 2 line unit of parent unit
Cat.3	Repairable on site by contractor's party (rep C) or returned to works or capable service unit (rep S)
Cat.4	Not repairable on site due to requirements for special equipment and/or facilities
Cat.5	Write off (Sub categories below)
Cat.5	(Components) Beyond economic repair, reduce to spares
Cat.5	(Scrap) Beyond economic repair or surplus to requirements. Dispose of or reduce to scrap
Cat.5	(Ground inst.) Beyond economic repair or surplus to requirements, but suitable for use as ground instructional airframe
Cat.5	(Missing) Failed to return

1941-1943 FAA:

S	Serviceable
X	Can be made serviceable by local resources
Y	Irreparable by local resources
Z	Likely to be struck off charge

1943-1944 FAA:

S	Serviceable
X1 A	Unserviceable but repairable within fourteen days
X2 A	Unserviceable but repairable by local resources outside fourteen days (sub Categories a, b, & c exist)
X/C	Unserviceable & requiring contractors working party
Y1 B	Major damage requiring return to repair yard or contractor
Y2 B	Deteriorated airframe, return to contractors for overhaul
Z	Total loss, struck off charge
Z1	Beyond economic repair, s.o.c & reduce to spares
Z2	Beyond economic repair, s.o.c & dispose as scrap

1944 onwards FAA:

SS	No damage
LQ	Light damage, Squadron repairable
LX	Light damage, Ship or airbase repairable
LC	Light damage but requiring contractors working party to repair on site
LY	Light damage not repairable by ship or airbase resources
HX	Heavy damage, Ship or airbase repairable
HC	heavy damage but requiring contractors working party to repair on site
HY	heavy damage not repairable by ship or airbase resources
ZZ	Lost or beyond economic repair

Aircraft Losses By Type & Date

Type	Ser/No	Date
Airspeed Oxford I	NM247	19/07/45
Armstrong Whitworth		
Albermarle II	V1711	13/03/44
Avro 504K	E3800	23/04/20
Avro Anson	G-AHFV	03/07/47
Avro Anson	G-AIWW	20/11/47
Avro Anson	K6246	06/01/40
Avro Anson T21	VV900	13/03/53
Avro Anson XIX	TX214	14/03/48
Avro Biplane	Unidentified	01/04/19
Avro Lancaster I	TW908	03/11/49
Avro Manchester 1	L7317	14/02/42
Blackburn Baffin	S1562	22/06/36
Blackburn Botha I	L6111	24/02/40
Blackburn Dart	S1129	11/03/29
Blackburn Dart T2	N9799	17/08/26
Blackburn Roc I	L3126	01/08/41
Blackburn Roc I	L3143	04/01/42
Blackburn Shark II	L2342	14/08/39
Blackburn Shark II	L2384	07/02/39
Blackburn Shark III	K8898	20/11/39
Blackburn Shark III	K8934	05/02/40
Boeing B-17	42-31149	31/12/43
Boeing B-17G	42-31064	30/12/43
Boulton Paul Defiant I	DR896	16/08/43
Bristol Beaufighter IF	V8265	09/09/42
Bristol Beaufighter IF	X7693	02/05/42
Bristol Beaufort I	L4475	08/03/40
Bristol Beaufort I	L9823	19/12/40
Bristol Blenheim 1F	T1804	24/08/40
Bristol Blenheim I	L4833	17/08/40
Bristol Blenheim I	L6686	22/12/40

Bristol Blenheim IV	L8793	25/09/40
Bristol Blenheim IV	L9455	20/05/40
Bristol Blenheim IV	P4837	20/05/40
Bristol Blenheim IV	V5396	22/03/41
Bristol Blenheim IVF	N3530	09/10/40
Bristol Hydroplane	None	15/04/13
Consolidated Catalina	VP-BPS	27/07/98
de Havilland Chipmunk	G-AMUD	22/03/53
de Havilland Chipmunk	G-ARME	29/03/66
de Havilland DH98A	G-AGPI	16/06/49
de Havilland Mosquito	Unidentified	23/07/46
de Havilland Mosquito FB VI	RF829	01/10/45
de Havilland Mosquito NF36	R1116	03/11/49
de Havilland Tiger Moth	Unidentified	07/11/50
de Havilland Tiger Moth L1	N9204	14/09/44
Dornier	Unidentified	05/05/42
Dornier Do 17P	Unidentified	11/07/40
Dornier Do 17P	Unidentified	15/08/40
Dornier Do 215 (?)	Unidentified	02/09/40
Dornier Do 217E-2	U5+GP	07/02/43
Dornier Do 217	Unidentified	04/05/42
Douglas Dakota	G-AGZB	06/05/62
Douglas Havoc	Unidentified	07/06/44
Fairey Albecore I	Bf634	07/11/42
Fairey Battle	K9230	28/04/41
Fairey Battle I	P2269	03/06/40
Fairey Firefly	Wd920	21/11/53
Fairey Firefly I	Z2046	01/03/45
Fairey Firefly IV	TW738	21/01/51
Fairey Fulmar I	N1924	11/06/41
Fairey Swordfish	K5983	26/09/39
Fairey Swordfish I	L7650	06/03/40
Fairey Swordfish I	L2769	19/09/39
Fairey Swordfish I	L2776	23/08/39
Fairey Swordfish II	DK687	09/03/42
Fairey Swordfish II	DK691	20/04/42
Fairey Swordfish II	HS313	07/03/43
Fairey Swordfish IIIF	NF333	11/10/45
Felixstowe F2A	N4499	15/05/24
Felixstowe F2A	N4570	12/12/23
Felixstowe F5	N4120	14/07/26
Gloster Gladiator	K7985	28/07/42
Gloster Gladiator II	L8030	28/07/42
Gloster Javelin Mk I	XA561	08/12/55

Gloster Meteor F4	VT233	22/04/49
Gloster Meteor F4	VW277	29/03/50
Grumman Martlett (Wildcat)	A1254	11/06/41
Handley-Page Halifax I	W7768	20/12/42
Handley-Page Halifax II	DK250	04/10/43
Handley-Page Halifax II	JD164	26/11/43
Handley-Page Hampden 1	AE397	14/02/42
Hawker Hunter F6	XF427	13/03/57
Hawker Hunter T8	Xl584	31/10/84
Hawker Hurricane	N3251	16/08/40
Hawker Hurricane	Unidentified	28/11/40
Hawker Hurricane I	L1770	28/09/40
Hawker Hurricane I	N2400	28/09/40
Hawker Hurricane I	P2720	07/11/40
Hawker Hurricane I	P2753	26/07/40
Hawker Hurricane I	P2770	07/11/40
Hawker Hurricane I	P2924	07/11/40
Hawker Hurricane I	P2947	08/08/40
Hawker Hurricane I	P2955	08/08/40
Hawker Hurricane I	P2957	08/08/40
Hawker Hurricane I	P2981	08/08/40
Hawker Hurricane I	P3058	08/08/40
Hawker Hurricane I	P3098	26/09/40
Hawker Hurricane I	P3163	08/08/40
Hawker Hurricane I	P3164	11/08/40
Hawker Hurricane I	P3167	27/10/40
Hawker Hurricane I	P3172	11/08/40
Hawker Hurricane I	P3267	08/08/40
Hawker Hurricane I	P3310	18/08/40
Hawker Hurricane I	P3381	08/08/40
Hawker Hurricane I	P3391	12/08/40
Hawker Hurricane I	P3468	08/08/40
Hawker Hurricane I	P3545	08/08/40
Hawker Hurricane I	P3617	08/08/40
Hawker Hurricane I	P3662	12/08/40
Hawker Hurricane I	P3681	11/07/40
Hawker Hurricane I	P3736	12/08/40
Hawker Hurricane I	P3764	13/08/40
Hawker Hurricane I	P3781	08/08/40
Hawker Hurricane I	P3823	08/08/40
Hawker Hurricane I	P3830	26/09/40
Hawker Hurricane I	P3836	28/09/40
Hawker Hurricane I	P3964	20/07/40
Hawker Hurricane I	P3973	21/07/40

Hawker Hurricane I	P5205	26/09/40
Hawker Hurricane I	R2683	07/11/40
Hawker Hurricane I	R4094	08/08/40
Hawker Hurricane I	R4176	12/08/40
Hawker Hurricane I	R4177	06/11/40
Hawker Hurricane I	R4180	12/08/40
Hawker Hurricane I	V6627	06/11/40
Hawker Hurricane I	V6691	28/11/40
Hawker Hurricane I	V6776	28/09/40
Hawker Hurricane I	V6888	27/10/40
Hawker Hurricane I	V6889	07/11/40
Hawker Hurricane I	V7294	11/08/40
Hawker Hurricane I	V7592	27/10/40
Hawker Hurricane II	BD940	22/11/41
Hawker Hurricane II	Z3396	23/06/41
Hawker Hurricane II	Z3899	22/11/41
Hawker Osprey	K3622	03/09/37
Hawker Osprey	K3631	05/03/35
Hawker Typhoon	JP844	05/11/43
Hawker Typhoon IB	DN303	29/05/43
Hawker Typhoon IB	MN735	07/06/44
Heinkel He 111	1G+AP	07/07/41
Heinkel He 111	1G+CC	08/05/41
Heinkel He 111	6N+GK	07/07/41
Heinkel He 111	6N+Hl	10/04/41
Heinkel He 111	Unidentified	14/08/40
Heinkel He 111	Unidentified	16/08/40
Heinkel He 111-H	G1+GK	26/09/40
Heinkel He 111-P	G1+GN	26/08/40
Heinkel He 59	Unidentified	08/08/40
Heinkel He 59	Unidentified	26/08/40
Heinkel He 111	Unidentified	09/09/42
Heinkel He 111	1G+AF	07/07/41
Junkers Ju87	S2+LM	08/08/40
Junkers Ju87	Unidentified	08/08/40
Junkers Ju87	Unidentified	08/08/40
Junkers Ju87	Unidentified	08/08/40
Junkers Ju87	Unidentified	08/08/40
Junkers Ju87	Unidentified	08/08/40
Junkers Ju87	Unidentified	08/08/40
Junkers Ju87	Unidentified	08/08/40
Junkers Ju87	Unidentified	18/08/40
Junkers Ju87	Unidentified	18/08/40
Junkers Ju87	Unidentified	18/08/40

Junkers Ju88	4D+CH	24/07/41
Junkers Ju88	7T+JH	30/05/41
Junkers Ju88	9K+AA	12/08/40
Junkers Ju88	9K+DL	19/09/40
Junkers Ju88	9K+F2	12/08/40
Junkers Ju88	9U+FR	19/08/40
Junkers Ju88	B3+LH	12/05/41
Junkers Ju88	M2+FH	19/08/42
Junkers Ju88	M7+EH	20/08/40
Junkers Ju88	Unidentified	12/08/40
Junkers Ju88	Unidentified	12/08/40
Junkers Ju88	Unidentified	12/08/40
Junkers Ju88	Unidentified	20/08/40
Junkers Ju88	Unidentified	20/08/40
Junkers Ju88	Unidentified	22/08/40
Junkers Ju88	Unidentified	23/08/40
Junkers Ju88D	4U+GH	25/08/42
Junkers Ju188	Z6+EX	18/04/44
Junkers Ju88A-1	F6+AM	27/04/41
Lockheed Avenger		
(Probably P-51)	Unidentified	10/02/45
Lockheed P-38	42-67456	22/07/44
Lockheed P-38	42-67943	22/07/44
Lockheed P-38	Unidentified	31/12/43
Lockheed P-38J-15-LO		
(Date Clash)	43-28702	27/11/43
Lockheed P-38	42-67943	22/07/44
Lockheed Ventura II	AE876	22/01/43
Martin Bf-26	42-96190	12/05/44
Messerschmitt Bf109	Black 1+	06/11/40
Messerschmitt Bf109	Grey 2+?	16/08/40
Messerschmitt Bf109	Unidentified	08/08/40
Messerschmitt Bf109	Unidentified	08/08/40
Messerschmitt Bf109	Unidentified	08/08/40
Messerschmitt Bf109	Unidentified	08/08/40
Messerschmitt Bf109	Unidentified	08/08/40
Messerschmitt Bf109	Unidentified	08/08/40
Messerschmitt Bf109	Unidentified	08/08/40
Messerschmitt Bf109	Unidentified	08/08/40
Messerschmitt Bf109	Unidentified	11/08/40
Messerschmitt Bf109	Unidentified	11/08/40
Messerschmitt Bf109	Unidentified	16/08/40
Messerschmitt Bf109	Unidentified	18/08/40
Messerschmitt Bf109	Unidentified	18/08/40

Messerschmitt Bf109	Unidentified	18/08/40
Messerschmitt Bf109	Unidentified	18/08/40
Messerschmitt Bf109	Unidentified	18/08/40
Messerschmitt Bf109	Unidentified	24/08/40
Messerschmitt Bf109	Unidentified	27/10/40
Messerschmitt Bf109	Unidentified	28/11/40
Messerschmitt Bf109	Unidentified	28/11/40
Messerschmitt Bf109	Unidentified	07/04/43
Messerschmitt Bf109	Yellow 6+	18/08/40
Messerschmitt Bf109	Yellow 8+?	15/10/40
Messerschmitt Bf109D	White 6+	18/08/40
Messerschmitt Bf109E	Unidentified	24/08/40
Messerschmitt Bf109E	Unidentified	25/08/40
Messerschmitt Bf109E	Unidentified	07/11/40
Messerschmitt Bf109E-4	Unidentified	25/07/40
Messerschmitt Bf109E	Unidentified	25/08/40
Messerschmitt Bf109F	Blue 4+	27/05/42
Messerschmitt Bf109G	Unidentified	16/08/43
Messerschmitt Bf109G-4	312+	14/09/43
Messerschmitt Bf110	3U+AR	26/09/40
Messerschmitt Bf110	5F+CM	26/09/40
Messerschmitt Bf110	MB+BP	15/08/40
Messerschmitt Bf110	MB+WP	15/08/40
Messerschmitt Bf110	U8+HH	26/09/40
Messerschmitt Bf110	Unidentified	08/08/40
Messerschmitt Bf110	Unidentified	08/08/40
Messerschmitt Bf110	Unidentified	15/08/40
Messerschmitt Bf110C-4	Unidentified	25/08/40
Messerschmitt Bf110C-4	Unidentified	25/08/40
Messerschmitt Bf110C-4Y	Unidentified	25/08/40
Messerschmitt Bf110D	Unidentified	01/10/40
Miles Monitor TT II	NP409	31/08/45
No.1 Seaplane	None	13/05/13
No.2 Seaplane	None	10/07/13
North American Harvard	Unidentified	09/06/47
North American P-51	44-13379	06/02/45
North American P-51	44-14383	06/02/45
North American P-51	AG389	20/01/43
North American P-51	FD508	02/12/43
Saunders-Roe Saro SR/A1	TG.271	12/08/49
Saunders-Roe Saro A33	K4773	25/10/38
Short Stirling III	EF311	28/08/44
Short Sunderland	NJ207	15/11/57
Short Sunderland Gr 5	VB885	13/02/46

Short Sunderland III	Ml725	19/11/47
Short Sunderland III	Ml789	28/01/53
Short Sunderland V	SZ565	16/11/51
Supermarine Scimitar FI	XD236	26/06/68
Supermarine Sea Otter ABR1	JM804	13/04/45
Supermarine Seafire 45	Unidentified	
Supermarine Spitfire I	R6631	28/11/40
Supermarine Spitfire	Unidentified	24/08/40
Supermarine Spitfire Iia	P7812	21/04/41
Supermarine Spitfire Mk I	K9882	26/09/40
Supermarine Spitfire Mk I	K9982	26/09/40
Supermarine Spitfire Mk I	K9990	18/07/40
Supermarine Spitfire Mk I	K9999	12/08/40
Supermarine Spitfire Mk I	L1082	24/08/40
Supermarine Spitfire Mk I	N3175	12/08/40
Supermarine Spitfire Mk I	N3239	24/08/40
Supermarine Spitfire Mk I	N3242	28/11/40
Supermarine Spitfire Mk I	P9333	12/08/40
Supermarine Spitfire Mk I	P9427	28/11/40
Supermarine Spitfire Mk I	P9456	12/08/40
Supermarine Spitfire Mk I	R6631	28/11/40
Supermarine Spitfire Mk I	X4016	16/08/40
Supermarine Spitfire Mk I	X4110	18/08/40
Supermarine Spitfire Mk I	X4586	28/11/40
Supermarine Spitfire Mk IIA	P7684	15/04/41
Supermarine Spitfire Mk IV	DP845	05/03/43
Supermarine Spitfire Mk IX	MJ219	11/06/44
Supermarine Spitfire Mk IX	MK323	11/11/44
Supermarine Spitfire Mk IX	NH183	07/06/44
Supermarine Spitfire Mk V	AB 208	16/06/44
Supermarine Spitfire Mk V	AD504	10/06/42
Supermarine Spitfire Mk V	AR377	10/06/42
Supermarine Spitfire Mk V	EN965	17/06/42
Supermarine Spitfire Mk VI	BR174	01/11/42
Supermarine Spitfire Mk VI	BR186	01/11/42
Supermarine Spitfire Mk XVI	S1553	21/02/48
Supermarine Spitfire PR 4	X4492	22/04/42
Supermarine Walrus I	L2335	27/06/45
Supermarine Walrus I	X9499	04/05/42
Supermarine Walrus I	X9518	04/05/42
Supermarine Walrus I	X9525	04/05/42
Supermarine Walrus I	X9554	04/05/42
Supermarine Walrus I	X9557	04/05/42
Supermarine Walrus I	X9558	04/05/42

Supermarine Walrus I	X9560	04/05/42
Taylorcraft	HH983	10/11/41
Unidentified British	Unidentified	08/11/40
Unidentified German	Unidentified	15/10/40
Unidentified German	Unidentified	13/03/41
Unidentified German	V4+AR?	05/04/41
Vickers Vampire	Unconfirmed	
Vickers Vildebeast	K4603?	21/08/39
Vickers Vildebeast	K6408	01/08/40
Vickers Wellington	Unidentified	06/12/41
Vickers Wellington IC	T2908	05/05/41
Westland Lysander III	T1439	20/09/41
Westland Wyvern	Wl887	28/03/57
Westland Wyvern	WP343	28/03/57
Whites Landplane	9841	07/09/16
Wight Quadruplane	None	01/09/16
Wight Quadruplane	None	31/03/17

Bibliography

Ashworth, Chris. *Action Stations 9*. Patrick Stephens Ltd. 1985

Barnes, C.H. *Shorts Aircraft since 1900*. Putnam Aeronautical. 1989

Beedle, J. 43 Squadron. Beaumont Aviation Literature. 1966

Bowyer, C. *The Short Sunderland*. Aston Publications Ltd. 1989

Bray, Peter. *Radar At Ventnor*. Ventnor local history society. 1989

Bray, Peter. *Ventnor area at war*. Ventnor local history society. 1989

Breslin, V.C. *History of The 20th Tactical F/ W*. 20th TFW History Office. 1990

Cantwell, Anthony. *Fort Victoria*. Isle of Wight County Council. 1985

Cooksley, Peter G. 1940 *The story of 11 Fighter Group*. Robert Hale Ltd. 1983

Chorley, W.R. *Bomber Command losses vol. 2*. Midland Counties Publications. 1994

Chorley, W.R. *Bomber Command losses vol. 3*. Midland Counties Publications. 1994

Chorley, W.R. *Bomber Command losses vol. 4*. Midland Counties Publications. 1996

Desmond, Kevin. *R Shuttleworth Biography*. Janes. 1982

Goodhall, Michael H. *The Wight Aircraft*. Gentry Books. 1973

Grattidge,Capt. H, *Captain of the Queens*. Oldbourne Press.

Gunston, Bill. *Bombers of WW2*. Salamander books. 1980

Halley, J.J. RAF *Aircraft serials L1000 – N9999*. Air Britain Publications.

Halley, J.J. RAF *Aircraft serials P1000 – R9999*. Air Britain Publications. 1996

Halley, J.J. RAF *Aircraft serials T1000 – V999*. Air Britain Publications. 1997

Halley, J.J. RAF *Aircraft serials W1000 – Z999*. Air Britain Publications. 1998

Halley, J.J. RAF *Aircraft serials BA100 – BZ999*. Air Britain Publications. 1985

Halley, J.J. RAF *Aircraft serials DA100 – DZ999*. Air Britain Publications. 1987

Halley, J.J. RAF *Aircraft serials EA100 – EZ999*. Air Britain Publications. 1988

Halley, J.J. RAF *Aircraft serials FA100 – FZ999*. Air Britain Publications. 1989

Halley, J.J. RAF *Aircraft serials MA100 – MZ999*. Air Britain Publications. 1991

Halley, J.J. RAF *Aircraft serials NA100 – NZ999*. Air Britain Publications. 1992

Halley, J.J. RAF *Aircraft serials PA100 – RZ999*. Air Britain Publications. 1992

Halley, J.J. RAF *Aircraft serials SA100 – VZ999*. Air Britain Publications. 1985

Halley, J.J. RAF *Aircraft serials XA100 – XZ999*. Air Britain Publications. 2001

Hough, R. & Richards, R. *Battle of Britain, Jubilee history*. Hodder & Stoughton. 1989

Houart, Victor. *Lonely Warrior*. Mayflower Paperbacks. 1969

Jenkins, P. & Shacklady, E. *Spitfire, The History*. Key Publishing. 1987

Ramsey, W. *Battle of Britain, Then & Now*. B.o.B. Prints International. 1985

Searle, Adrian. *I.O.W. At War*. Dovecote Press. 1989

Smith, Peter C. *Stuka at War*. Ian Allen Ltd. 1989

Sturtivant, R & Burrow M. *Fleet Air Aircraft* 1939-1945. Air Britain Publications. 1995

Sturtivant, R. *The Anson File*. Air Britain Publications. 1988

Tagg, A.E. & Wheeler, R.L. *From Sea to Air*. Crossprint. 1989

Thompson, D. & Sturtivant, R. *RAF Aircraft serials J1-J9999*. Air Britain Publications. 1987

Various. *The Encylopedia of Air Warfare*. Salamander books. 1975

Various. *75 Eventful Years*. Wingham Aviation Books. 1993

Magazines, Periodicals and other Publications

Isle of Wight County Press

Flypast

Flying Review International

339th Fighter Group Newsletter

Aeroplane Monthly

A short History of Somerton Airport

Worcester Polytechnic Journal; Winter 1995

HMSO. Civil aircraft accident reports Nos:

MCAP.33	1947
MCAP.47.	1948
MCAP.48.	1948
MCAP.83.	1950
MCAP.C612.	1953
MCAP.149.	1958
MCAP.197.	1963
MCAP.274.	1967
MCAP.C609	1953

Glossary

A7AEE	Aeroplane & Armaments Experimental Establishment.
AA	Anti-Aircraft
AACU	Anti-Aircraft Co-operation Unit
A.F.C.	Air Force Cross
ASR	Air Sea Rescue
ASTE	Air Services Training Establishment
ATC	Air Training Corps
ATDU	Aircraft Torpedo Development Unit
BOAC	British Overseas Airways Corporation
DFC	Distinguished Flying Cross
DFM	Distinguished Flying Medal
EFTS	Elementary Flight Training Unit
ETA	Estimated Time of Arrival
FAA	Fleet Air Arm
FIR	Flight Information Region
FRADU	Fleet Requirement & Direction Unit
FRAeS	Fellow of the Royal Aeronautical Society
FTU	Flying Training Unit
GSU	Group Service Unit
HMS	Her/His Majestys Ship
IAS	Indicated Air Speed
IWCP	*Isle of Wight County Press*
MU	Maintenance Unit
NDB	Non-Directional Beacon
NFS	National Fire Service
OCU	Operational Conversion Unit
OTU	Operational Training Unit
POW	Prisoner of War
QMS	Quarter Master Sergeant
RAAF	Royal Australian Air Force
RAF	Royal Air Force
RAFVR	Royal Air Force Volunteer Reserve
RCAF	Royal Canadian Air Force
RNAS	Royal Naval Air Service (or Station)
RNLI	Royal National Lifeboat Institution

ROC	Royal Observer Corps
S.D.F.	Special Duties Flight
SOC	Struck Off Charge
TFW	Tactical Fighter Wing
TOC	Taken Off Charge
TTU	Torpedo Training Unit
WOC	Written Off Charge
Wk Nr	Werkbild Nummer (works number)